SINGLE UNTIL...

STRATEGIES FOR STANDING ON THE PROMISES OF GOD WHILE IN SOLITUDE

Shajuana R. Ditto

ISBN 978-1-0980-7017-5 (paperback)
ISBN 978-1-0980-7018-2 (digital)

Christian Faith Publishing, Inc.
832 Park Avenue
Meadville, PA 16335
www.christianfaithpublishing.com

Printed in the United States of America

Contents

Preface

Jesus, I love You! I thank You for taking the time out just to hear my heart's cry in this season of my life. Right now, God, I pray that You bless every person that reads through this devotion. I pray that in the next couple of days, our eyes stay fixed on You and our hearts are open to what You would have to say. Lord, You are good! You are good in the good times, in the bad times, and the ugliest times of our lives, and I thank You. I pray that You breathe upon the words that are in this devotional and allow Your breath to speak to the dry bones of our singleness.

Father, I pray that every young girl that reads this is empowered and encouraged in this time. I pray that her heart is open. I pray that she finds her worth in You. For every young guy that may skim through these pages, I pray that he will find a mentor that will speak life over him into his singleness. Thank You that even in the most desperate times, You were there.

Lord, I thank You for keeping my mind and my heart sound in this season. I pray that You continue to cover all the single people in this season. May Your favor be upon us and a thousand generations. I pray that in this time of solitude, we are rest assured that You are calling us back to Your heart. You are calling us back to purity. You are calling us back to holiness.

Now, Lord, I pray that we say *yes* to Your will, *yes* to Your way, and *yes* to Your Word. In Jesus's name, amen.

Acknowledgments

To my parents who believed in me and never pressured me to be someone that I am not, I thank you. Thank you for modeling a kingdom marriage and encouraging me in my singleness. My prayer is throughout these pages, this next generation will feel empowered and encouraged in this season. To the most amazing friends that a girl could have, thank you for supporting me in this season of my singleness. It is because of you that I am able to keep a sound mind during this time of preparation. To Generation Z and the millennials reading this, I pray you understand we have a responsibility to love God and to love others. Marriage is not for everyone and being single is not for everyone. God accepts you and loves you and will meet you wherever you are in life because He died for everyone. I believe God will bless this season of waiting. I refuse to settle for less than God's best, and I encourage you to do the same.

Introduction

Rick Warren said, "God is love. He didn't need us. But He wanted us. And that is the most amazing thing." One thing is for certain, everyone wants to have love and wants to be loved. The desire and agape love that Jesus has for us should give us hope. God loves us so much that He gave His only begotten Son. The ultimate sacrifice was made because you and I are wanted. There are different words in the Greek and Hebrew that relate to love. Agape is the Hebrew word of love meaning self-less love or Christian love. Agape love is sacrificial. Agape love keeps on giving and giving no matter what. Agape love is not based on feelings or emotions. Agape love doesn't expect anything in return.

One thing I love about the Word of God is it is real and relevant and can bring much resolve and peace into your life, especially if you are single. God has a special place in His heart for His people. Singleness is not a curse or a disease. Let me apologize for every person that ever made you feel as though you were not good enough because of your status of being single. Personally, I have been in that very place. A place of judgement. I am well into my thirties, in ministry, and I am not married and have no children. God has been teaching me about finding my identity in Him and in Him alone. Can I encourage you today? Your identity isn't wrapped up in your current status or your past. The goal is for you and I to begin to develop healthy habits that affirm who we are in Christ.

Throughout the pages of this devotional, you will definitely get a feel for my personality. I wanted to write this devotional for "my kids" aka my students. I have had the awesome privilege of coaching over one hundred student-athletes and speaking life over youth and young adults across the world. Building relationships over the past few years has helped me discover one common theme: everyone wants to be wanted, accepted, seen and to feel valued. Being single can be devastating. And I believe that God has literally placed me in a position to encourage and inspire the next generation of having a kingdom mindset when it comes to being single. There have been times I have had to encourage myself in my singleness. Your singleness can either define you, distract you or develop you for such a time as this. Living in a small town, I feel, at times, like I am out of place. The demographic of the churches I have attended are majorly family focused. I want to encourage you in this moment to find your community. Your community is a huge necessity and clutch in getting you through your current season. The right people need to be in the right place for you to have the right perspective about your relationships. For us to come into true obedience to our purpose we must have the right people.

You will read in the upcoming pages about my story and my vow to purity. I made up my mind at a very young age that I want to be different. I want to do things the "right way," and not only the right way but God's way. Everyone's "right way" may look different. Again, my story is not your story. I do believe we have to recognize our past, seek God's forgiveness and realize what is pleasing to the Lord. According to Romans 3:23-25 we have all fallen short of the glory of God. I want it to be clear and evident that we serve a forgiving and faithful God. Also, He is a God of detail and order. Not only a detailed God but a God of restoration. Jeremiah 29:11 declares that He has plans for us. Plans to prosper us and not to harm us. The only person we have to please and the only opinion that matters is that of our Heavenly Father. So, I wanted to write a devotional for the fourteen-year-old me. I know there will be a plethora of individuals who will grab a copy just to support me. Please, do me a favor; wrap this devotional book up as a gift to your teen niece or nephew. I wish I had someone just encouraging me that I was doing the right thing. I wish I had a *Chicken Soup for the Soul* book that spoke to the future me about how to deal with singleness in your thirties. Not only my thirties but my pre-teens. There was no one creating a culture of positive reinforcements of healthy boundaries. The body of Christ and the culture failed in helping us release relationships that did more harm than good. The microwave generation that we live in today is unfortunate. The art of communication has been lost and it is problematic even in our personal relationship with Christ.

I wish I had a mentor to speak life over me when I was in my teens. Now, I have the awesome honor of doing just that. Youth and young adults have always been a passion of mine since I was young. When I was twelve years old, I knew what I wanted to do. I wanted to coach. The coach inside of me loves to encourage. The coach inside of me loves to discipline when necessary.

I love winning, and I hate losing. I enjoy going into the locker room, motivating my players when we are down by two. The most rewarding thing I love about coaching is I get to mentor. I get to mentor young females and wear the hat of a big sister, momma bear, teacher, youth pastor, and so much more. I don't take the call on my life lightly. This next generation is struggling with their worth, value, self-confidence and identity. I want to be a resource and a beacon of hope, especially for those who are going through the season of singleness.

In the next few pages, I want to be your singleness coach. I want to call a timeout in your life, and I want to motivate you. I want to encourage you if you are struggling right now in your singleness. I want to help you get a strategy against the opponent (Satan), and I want to help you win. These pages reflect my personal testimony while single. Throughout the course of time, I have grown so much in my relationship with Christ. That's my whole goal, I want to help you grow closer to Christ. I want you to know how valuable you are in His sight. Again, singleness is not a curse, and you are not alone. We all need a strategy for life. That strategy comes from the best book you will ever read, and that is the Word of God. Kingdom singleness must be built on kingdom principles. You ready? Stay single until…

Single Until...

Pastor Tony Evans once said, "*a kingdom marriage is a covenantal union between a man and a woman who commit themselves to function in unison under divine authority in order to replicate God's image and expand His rule in the world through both their individual and joint callings.*" Simply put, Pastor Evans explained that the mission for marriage is to

1. Reflect the image of God;
2. Advance God's kingdom on Earth.

I reached out to a couple of my single friends, and I posed this question: "Why do you want to get married?" Not only was I curious, but I wanted to check my heart. I wanted to make sure my motive was pure and *of* God. The answers that my friends sent did not surprise me. I know their hearts' desires and their pure intentions when it comes to marriage. Unanimously, all of them desire to have someone they can *do* life with. All of them want children and their families to grow in unity under the authority of Jesus Christ. If we are honest with ourselves, we are so focused on the wedding day that we miss the sole purpose of marriage. We must understand that the wedding is just one day, but the marriage is a whole lifetime until death do you part. Marriage is more than our happiness, sexual gratification, and companionship. It is a covenant that mirrors and honors God's covering and the love He has for us.

"*When you eat or drink or do anything else, always do it to honor God*" *(1 Corinthians 10:31).*

The hardest conversation I had was with my parents. I told my parents that I did not want to get married! I know that they were disappointed. I know their hearts dropped into their stomachs. I will never ever forget the reaction on their faces. Right now, some of you reading this are shocked! Calm down! When I told my parents, it was like I had robbed them of becoming grandparents. Or maybe they were fearful of my future of being by myself for the rest of my life. And that was not my intention at all.

For the past five years, my parents ask me the same question over and over again. "When can we get some grandkids?"

My answer is always the same. "When I get a husband!" Please, understand, I am not giving up on God. I am not speaking death over my future relationships. I have not stopped praying for the man of God that He has for me. However, I do not want to get married if I am *not* honoring or pleasing God right now in this season. My motive for marriage can't be based on one thing—to have kids for my parents to be grandparents. Not only that, but we serve a God of order. I need who God has for me to be sensitive to God's voice and surrendered to God's plan. Unfortunately, the culture that we live in has a total opposite approach of honoring God through relationships. We want the *likes*, we live in a society that's more focused on the approval of people with social media being the catalyst to this fix. How many likes will I get? What does it matter if we don't have the stamp or the approval from God himself? Does Jesus approve your post on social media? Does Jesus approve of the relationship that you are currently in? We need the stamp of approval from Jesus Christ and not man. I definitely recommend you read Pastor Mike Todd's book *Relationship Goals* for practical steps for relationship growth. But this unwanted culture pressure will drive us to settle for just anyone, and I refuse to settle. I want to be a woman after God's own heart.

I want to ask my single friends, this next generation, and people in relationships that if Jesus isn't at the foundation of our relationships, what would the outcome be? This, my friends, is where this devotional was birthed. I will remain *single until* my motive *for* marriage aligns with the biblical principles *of* marriage. I've had friends call me "holier than thou" and "too deep" when it comes to godly order in my singleness. And I am okay with that! I will never be about people pleasing. I will continue to press forward and please God. Be encouraged today to stop worrying about what people think of you and your current status.

Your challenge this week: Ask your friends why they want to get married. Then, ask yourself, "What is my motive for getting married?" #SingleUntil.

Reflection Page

Single Until: Challenge/ Confirmation/ Change

My challenge:

Make a list of other's expectations that challenge you in your singleness.

My confirmation for today:

(Start with an *I am* statement.) What is the Lord speaking to you in your singleness right now?

Change:

Write some things you wish you could change in your life while dealing with being single.

Your future needs a foundation.

Movement, Moment, and Mirror

God is raising a generation of singles who are content and confident in their relationship with Christ. Not only are we confident and content, we may have even become comfortable in being by ourselves. The most important factor that we should understand is this is the perfect moment to become who God is calling us to be. I am not encouraging you to stay content or comfortable. We serve a God who moves and wants you to constantly grow! Comfort zones were not designed by God. Growth and being comfortable can't coexist. I do not want you to think for one moment that I am encouraging you to be by yourself and stay by yourself for the rest of your life. I am saying, however, that God is raising up singles in this season to encourage the next generation that Jesus is all we need until He brings the right people into our lives.

God is raising up a generation of people who are single and who have postured themselves in submission to the Holy Spirit. Our hearts' posture is in such a significant place right now that our eyes are fixated on Christ and Christ alone. It is a new day and a new era. This is the *movement* for the singles across this nation; our hearts, minds, and eyes are fixed on Jesus. We have so many movements in our culture today that we should take pride in the fact that God is trying to mold us into being whomever He wants us to be without any distractions. While in our singleness, God is able to use the lonely, depressed and anxious nights for our good. God will always flip the script to set you up for success in your singleness. You can stand on God's promises, believe in God's purpose and pursue the kingdom plan God has for your life. Right now, in your singleness, there is a movement taking place. No, I am not talking about a pledge or hashtag, but I am talking about a divine *moment* that is aligning your heart with the heart of God. You will miss this moment if you are distracted with the wrong person, the wrong perspective, or the wrong heart posture. God is on the verge of blessing the singles that are not only waiting on a spouse but desiring to become like the bride of Christ. God is about to turn your most lonely days into some of your most blessed days as you read throughout this devotion. Have your cried? I'm sure. Have you given up hope? Possibly! But if you are reading this, you are right where the Lord wants you to be. God is telling singles across this nation that the wait will be worth it.

How do I know if I am still single myself? I must believe that the Word of God is true and will not return void! I do believe that, as singles, we have positioned ourselves for such a time as this to find our identity and purity in Christ. Do I have the answers in finding your future spouse? No, ma'am. No, sir! This devotional may not be for you. But it is for this next generation who has aligned their hearts with God's will. If you are single, God wants you to stand on the Word of God and not to waiver.

Being single you must focus on the movement, moment, and the mirror. As you walk past the mirror, reflect on all the negative things you have ever said to yourself. I want you to reevaluate what God says about you and write those down. As someone who is single, I have said some of the most disrespectful things to myself. In this season, God has shown me a couple of things concerning my relationships with other people, and I need to fix those broken relationships, toxic behaviors and forgive, so that I can move forward in my future relationships. God wants us to be a reflection of Him in every aspect of our lives. The enemy tried to make us feel as though we weren't good enough in our singleness, but today, we tell the devil that his time is up and that God is enough. Singles, it's time to *grow* in Christ. Don't miss this moment with God; don't miss this movement with God, and as people see you, I pray that we are mirroring our future relationships with that of the one we have with Christ Jesus.

Your challenge for the week: write "*I am*" statements on Post-it notes or note cards and place them around your room. Every morning, when you wake up, declare out loud your "*I am*" statements. Start with "*I am not alone!*"

Reflection Page

Single Until: Challenge/Confirmation/Change

My challenge:

Make a list of things that challenge you in your singleness.

My confirmation for today:

(Start with an *I am* statement.) What is the Lord speaking to you in your singleness right now?

Change:

Write some things you wish you could change in your life while dealing with being single.

God will step in when you step out of the way! Are you trying to get ahead of God? Does God have total control over your life in this season of singleness?

"Good because He Is God"

For we are His workmanship,
created in Christ Jesus for good works, which God prepared
beforehand, that we should walk in them.

—Ephesians 2:10

If you don't get anything else out of this devotion, write this on a sticky note, and write this with a permanent marker on your bathroom mirror: "I am good because He is God!" Let that get in your spirit today. I am *good* because He is God! No matter what your last relationship looked like, or whatever lie the enemy is placing in your mind right now, again, you are good because He is God! Many of us think that we are not good enough.

The enemy has planted lies in our head about: the way we look, our past, and the guilt we should feel for something that has happened five years ago. Shame continues to knock on your door, and you continue to open. You've listened to the lies so much, you started to believe it!

It doesn't matter if you are male or female, sixteen or sixty; at one point, you have looked in the mirror and have listened to those horrible lies concerning you! Well, today, those lies stop! Begin to change the way you speak to your inner self! Begin to "change your language" around your day to day life. Instead of talking doubt, start speaking deliverance over yourself. Instead of speaking fear, begin to quote *faith* scriptures that will help you move those mountains of unforgiveness, doubt, and shame. Change the language of worry into unrehearsed worship. The Bible says, "Whatever a man thinks, so is he!" Could it be you are attracting the wrong person because of the very thoughts you are thinking about yourself?

Please know that you can carry yourself with confidence and still be battling with insecurity! You can be frustrated in this season and still have faith in God. God is not calling you to be perfect! As a matter of fact, He is looking for the vulnerable and the weak. Second Corinthians 12:9 says His power is made perfect in our weakness. He wants all of you! He wants our mess, our brokenness, our self-doubt, and every insecurity that paralyzes our purpose! He wants all of it! And once we give it to God, let's take the necessary steps to heal and grow in the direction of our destiny. Repeat after me: "I am validated by Jesus Christ!" Your validation comes from Jesus Christ and Him alone!

Declare Palm 26 over your life:

> Vindicate me, O Lord, for I have walked in my integrity; I have relied on and trusted confidently in the Lord without wavering and I shall not slip! Examine me, O Lord, and try me; test my heat and my mind. For your lovingkindness is before my eyes, and I have walked faithfully in your truth.

When you look in the mirror this week, change the way you think about yourself! Decree, "I am good because He is God."

Affirmation for the day: I am God's workmanship! I am *good* because He is God!

Reflection Page

Single Until: Challenge/Confirmation/Change

My challenge:

Make a list of things that challenge you in your singleness.

My confirmation for today:

(Start with an *I am* statement.) What is the Lord speaking to you in your singleness right now?

Change:

Write some things you wish you could change in your life while dealing with being single.

Attracted and Distracted

Today, during my quiet time, God asked me if He was good enough for me. I literally remember pausing for a moment while I was writing in my journal because it was so audible and so profound! Let me push pause right here because I want to be very clear to this next generation. God still *speaks*! Of course, God is good enough for me! I then heard, "Prove it!"

Now, the question I have for you is will you be okay if God calls you to a lifetime of being single? Many of you are hyperventilating right now. Calm down! It's just a question! What if God calls you to be single right now in this moment of your life? What if you get convicted so much after this time that you break up with your distractions? Is it possible that God is calling you back to His presence, His Word, and His heart in this time of being by yourself? Your singleness is between you and God. What you do in this season of your singleness, again, is between you and God, not social media and definitely not between people who shouldn't be speaking into your life in the first place.

When I heard Holy Spirit say, "Prove that I am enough for you," I knew that it was going to take some action on my part. Discipline is a hard word to swallow in your singleness. But how bad do you want the things of God? I believe we misinterpret a lot of scriptures in our singleness! I am not a Bible scholar nor am I theologian, and I do not pretend to be. I am not a counselor nor am I a psychiatrist. Listen, I am just a country girl living in this world, trying to figure out how to live this single life that will be pleasing to God. Again, this devotion is set up to help singles strategize in this time of solitude. After much prayer and asking the Holy Spirit for wisdom, I just placed pen to paper. So if for some odd reason your heart is beating really fast or sweat has made its way to your upper lip, just breathe. I am standing with you that God has someone for you.

One scripture that we respectively and repeatedly quote is 1 Corinthians 7: "It is better to be single, for it is better to marry than to burn with passion!" I honestly do not believe that God wants us to "*do*" life by ourselves! When it comes to your singleness, I believe that God will place people around you to get you through those times of loneliness. Let me be completely honest with you; I have found myself distracted by the things most attractive! Not only the opposite sex, but houses, cars, and the next step in my career. I want whatever God has for me, of course. Have you ever found your eyes wandering and wanting what someone else has? I do believe that when something looks good, the enemy has a profound way of making us think that we need that in our life. Remember, everything that looks good is not always good for us! We must have discipline in this season. We must work at our relationship with Jesus Christ.

If you find yourself going back-and-forth with wanting to be in a relationship, you're not crazy; that is perfectly normal. It's like a roller coaster; one day, you want to be in a relationship. The next day, you're like, "Yep, God, I am good!" You may be in a season in which you are at peace with being by yourself. You can also be in a season where you are desperate and lonely, and you are doing things that are not pleasing to God! Call a time-out in your life right now! Figure out which season you are in! Ask God to give you a peace in whatever season that may be! This is a really bold prayer that I prayed: "Lord, if I am not supposed to be in a relationship right now, take the desire away from me!" Jesus did just that! I have total peace in my singleness right now! Does that mean that I am called to be single? No, but God is good enough for me! To know the desires of God's heart, you must have the discipline to follow God's plan! Is God good enough for you? Prove it!

Reflection Page

To know the desires of God's heart,
you must have the discipline to follow God's plan.

Single Until: Challenge/Confirmation/Change

My challenge:

Make a list of things that challenge you in your singleness.

My confirmation for today:

(Start with an *I am* statement.) What is the Lord speaking to you in your singleness right now?

Change:

Write some things you wish you could change in your life while dealing with being single.

*To know the desires of God's heart, you must
have the discipline to follow God's plan.*

"Desperate Times Call for Desperate Measures"

Now may the God of peace himself sanctify you completely,
and may your whole spirit and soul and body be kept
blameless at the coming of our Lord Jesus Christ.
—1 Thessalonians 5:23

In 2017, I was praying for my future husband. I would write down prayers for my husband to read once we met each other! If you are single, I encourage you to start a prayer journal just for your spouse. This would be a great gift on the day of your wedding. Now, I have about two journals and over one hundred letters! It is now three years later. After cleaning out my desk, I opened up this particular letter because I wanted to see what I had prayed. I started all my letters off the same:

> *Dear Future Husband,*
> *I am almost 30! I told God that if I wasn't in a relationship by 30, then I get it, I am supposed to be single! Because I am getting really comfortable here in this season! I had a revelation today however! Are you ready? "Maybe God hasn't sent you to me because I'm not desperate enough for HIM…" I never want my motive to be in a relationship to be because everyone else is! I don't believe that's the way the Lord operates! He checks our hearts—and my motive is worldly! I am in a desperate place (keep in mind this was 2017.) I'm in a desperate place*

for you and becoming your wife and neglecting my place as His daughter! Love you, though! Today, I am praying for you! Today, I pray that God will give you guidance and strength! Today, I pray that if you are just as discouraged as me that God will give you the comfort and strength that only He can give!

Love, your future wife!

Desperation for Jesus is knowing that He exists in our lives, but we want more of Him and less of the world. More of His presence. More of His power. More of His anointing in our life. *"Oh, let me rise in the morning and live always with you" (Psalm 139:18)*. We find David who is desperate to know of God! If you recall, David was a "man after God's own heart." This type of recognition can only be constructed by his level of desperation. We must be desperate for the Word of God! We need to be so desperate for the Word that we are not led astray by false teaching! Desperation for Jesus will help you have a Mark 5 moment. You will begin to recognize your issues in your own life and push yourself through a crowd just to touch a piece of His clothing to be healed from any addiction, lustful thoughts, past afflictions, or pride. One author writes, "If we don't feel desperate for God, we don't tend to cry out to Him. This leads to spiritual death."

"Search me, O God, and know my heart; test me and know my anxious thoughts. See if there is any offensive way in me, and lead me in the way everlasting" (Psalms 139:23–24).

If you are feeling desperate in this time of singleness, reexamine yourself at this time. Are you more desperate for relationships right now that you are not working on your personal relationships with Jesus Christ? Desperate times call for desperate measures! It is time for you to ask God to reveal who you are in Him!

Reflection Page

Single Until: Challenge/Confirmation/Change

My challenge:

Make a list of things that challenge you in your singleness.

My confirmation for today:

(Start with an *I am* statement.) What is the Lord speaking to you in your singleness right now?

Change:

Write some things you wish you could change in your life while dealing with being single.

Rizpah, Rapunzel, and Rahab

Never give up on something that you can't
go a day without thinking about.
—Winston Churchill

In 2 Samuel 3:7, we find a woman named Rizpah. I want us to focus today on her name! Rizpah's name means "coal" and "hot stone!" Rizpah is a woman of desperation. If you have the time, please, read into Rizpah's story because it is pretty amazing. If you are a single mom reading this, I encourage you to highlight and dive into the story in 2 Samuel. Even if you aren't a single mom, read this story. My audience for this whole devotional revolves around teenage girls. So even if you do not identify with Rizpah, you may see yourself as the modern-day Rapunzel.

My students are very familiar with Rapunzel. Here are some particulars associated with Rizpah. She is Mephibosheth's mother. She is Saul's concubine (2 Samuel 3:7). A famine hit Israel for three years (2 Samuel 21:6), and Rizpah's sons were hung (2 Samuel 21:8–9). Rizpah stays upon a rock where her sons were hung for five months because she did not want birds to devour her sons bodies (2 Samuel 21:10).

Some of you are saying, "This has nothing to do with me." So let me deliver Rizpah's profile. Rizpah is a mother, sees herself as useless, found herself in the struggle but came out on top, she is grieving, and she is desperate. Here me out; this is for the ones who hung up their dreams, put their purpose on the back burner, hung up the vison God gave, and threw their whole career away because God hasn't promoted them or advanced them yet. Can you imagine sleeping on a rock like Rizpah did out of desperation? Can you imagine lying in the rain to protect someone that you loved?

Maybe you feel like you've lost in this season of singleness. Everyone is getting married and engaged, and here you are, in a desperate moment. Have you placed marriage and being in a relationship at such a high priority that you are forgetting the ministry that God has placed before you? I can see Rizpah in her situation. I can see her in quiet time with Jesus, pleading for Him to take the pain away. Make sure you read the scripture in 2 Samuel as soon as you can! She's on this rock, making sure that her sons don't get eaten by birds. I can see her taking whatever is around her and using it to make sure that nothing harmed her child. Right now, in your life, what are you using around you to protect your—dreams, passions, and purpose?

On rainy days, I imagine Rizpah being on the rock where her sons were lying, her head pressed on her hands, crying out to God to give her strength. I can see her on some lonely nights, being scared of being by herself. Can you identify with Rizpah? I sure can! I have found myself with my head pressed in my hands, crying. I have aborted dreams and visions because of feeling inadequate. I have had some lonely nights where only God could be my comfort and strength and catch every tear that was rolling down my face. I believe that we will all go through this process. I don't want you to focus on the fact that you may not have children, but imagine lying on a rock for five months. Lonely, desperate, and over life, you must find strength in knowing that you have to protect the very thing that you love.

For the younger audience, let's think about the Disney character, Rapunzel. Rapunzel is classified as "the maiden in the tower." Rapunzel is known for the line, "Rapunzel, Rapunzel, let down your hair." Even though Rapunzel was in a tower, just waiting for someone to rescue her, I can only think that she too had some difficult days of being by herself. As she let down her hair, I can imagine her letting her guard down. I can see her giving up in her most vulnerable moments of life. Is this you?

Maybe you can't identify with the woman named Rizpah or the fictional character of Rapunzel. There leaves one more woman mentioned in the Bible named Rahab. She was single, *single*. The millennials will understand what I am saying. Rahab was loyal, and she was obedient. What people know most about Rahab is that she was a prostitute. Her bio is in Joshua 2. Read that tonight, for sure.

Rahab, Rapunzel, and Rizpah all have something in common. They all found themselves in desperate situations. Not only that, they fought for their livelihood while being single. They did not allow any situation or title define whose they were. All three ladies probably wanted to give up, but they didn't. God is saying to you today, "Don't you dare give up!" This week, I want you to write a couple of things that you have given up on. Maybe you've even given up on yourself. I want you to write some things down that are around you right now that can be used to protect your purpose. Single for five months, ten months, or your whole entire existence—you must protect your peace and purpose and gain strength and power while waiting on the Lord while single!

Reflection Page

Single Until: Challenge/Confirmation/Change

My challenge:

Make a list of things that challenge you in your singleness.

My confirmation for today:

(Start with an *I am* statement.) What is the Lord speaking to you in your singleness right now?

Change:

Write some things you wish you could change in your life while dealing with being single.

Closet Doors

Come near to God and He will come near to you!
—James 4:8

Singles, I want to encourage you right now to clean out your closets today! I need you to have a "war room" experience in your life and create a space where it is just you and God! I want to encourage you to pursue the presence of God. There have been many instances in my life that what I have prayed in private, God had shown His favor in public.

In James 4:8, we are encouraged that when we come near to God, He will come near to us. In your most discouraging moments, get in the closet. When you are over your singleness or dealing with your heart being in broken pieces, draw near to God. When you're feeling overwhelmed, go to your secret place. Cleaning out your closet may not be something you feel like doing. I get it! But I do want to encourage you to find a quiet secret place where you can seek the presence of God. For further reading, please read *Mark 1:35-37, "Very early in the morning, while it was still dark, Jesus got up, left the house and went off to a solitary place."*

I can imagine some of your faces right now. "I'm not getting up at 6:00 a.m. to find a solitary place to talk to God." If you are desperate enough, you will! Think about it this way: if you can get up at 5:00 a.m. to go stand in line at your favorite store on Black Friday, you will definitely do whatever it takes to spend time with God if it is important to you! We always make time for the things that are important to us. Maybe, your solitary place is in your car, at your desk, or in the locker room before school. Wherever your solitary place is, I want you to start positioning your heart so that God may speak to you in a different way.

Desperation in the *Oxford Dictionary* is defined as "of a person having a great need or desire for something." I told myself that I was going to meet with Jesus in my prayer closet every night at 7:00 p.m.! Life happened, and my job became a top priority. Coaching volleyball became my second priority. The 7:00 p.m. then became 9:00 p.m.; 9:00 p.m. then became "I'll do it tomorrow!" My great need was being validated by other people. My great need was gratification from my career. True maturity is evident when God's need is your need. When the Lord becomes your Shephard and you shall not be in want of things of the world you have reached the capacity of true spiritual growth. We live in a generation that is concerned with two things: *self* and *excuses*. If it doesn't benefit us in any way, we don't want it. We have the "I'll do it tomorrow" mentality. God is calling us back to a solitary and secret place. There are revelations that God wants to reveal to us in this time. But because we are lazy in the body of Christ, and because God is not a priority in our lives, we place Him last on our to-do list. I get it; we are human, but if we can make time to post a story on Instagram, if we can make Snapchat streaks a priority, surely, we can spend some time with our Lord and Savior.

You need this time in your singleness to be empowered. I am the most vulnerable in my closet! Why? Because I know the Lord will not judge me! I am the most transparent in my secret place. Why? Because I know that there are strategies for my singleness in my secret place.

"Here I am! I stand at the door and knock. If anyone hears my voice and opens the door, I will come in and eat with that person, and they with me" (Revelation 3:20).

Who is knocking at your door right now? Is depression knocking? Fear knocks really loud. Have you answered that door in your singleness? Is doubt peeking through your window? As you *position* your heart to receive what God has for you, He will begin to eliminate distractions and pull you close to His heart. He will tell you what door to open and what door to shut. But it all starts in your secret place.

Reflection Page

Single Until: Challenge/Confirmation/Change

My challenge:

Make a list of things that challenge you in your singleness.

My confirmation for today:

(Start with an *I am* statement.) What is the Lord speaking to you in your singleness right now?

Change:

Write some things you wish you could change in your life while dealing with being single.

Your purpose does not revolve around people.

Pressure Points

Singleness is a mindset that either helps you grow or makes you go crazy! Can someone please tell me where in the Bible it says that I have to be married by twenty-five, two kids by twenty-seven, homeowner by thirty, and thriving in my career by thirty-five? It doesn't! I hate when people ask, "When are you going to get married, when are you going to have children? Why aren't you in a relationship yet?" Having standards, having high expectations and setting boundaries should be commended. How dare we show up to events without a date! Weddings and family functions seem to be the worst! And don't you dare have the audacity to bring just "a *friend*" or some of your single friends with you. Jesus Himself should come back right then and there when you step foot in these events by yourself. Take the pressure off.

People seem appalled when you come strolling in with one of your best friends! How does one answer that question? Why are you still single? For some, it is a choice that they are making! Maybe some of us are working on who God has called us to be. Maybe we are making room for our future spouses by trying to heal some deep wounds. Maybe we are getting the counseling needed, attending single conferences in preparation for our future relationships! Some, well, we are waiting for the perfect person to come knocking on our door!

The Word of God says that He gives us the desires of our hearts! So if your desire is to be married, then continue to believe that God is going to do just what He said—give you the desires of your heart! The next time people ask the daunting questions—"Aren't you ready to be married? Why are you still single?"—just tell them you are waiting on the Lord! I mean that's the best advice I could give any-one! Why not wait a little while longer? I'd rather be with God's best than God's busted! I just want to encourage you in this moment; take the pressure off! If you are believing that God has someone tailor-made just for you, then keep believing!

Are you ready for the question of the day? Are you afraid of being alone? Many people settle in life because they just can't stand the thought of being alone. They rush into relationships because they are afraid of the season of loneliness. "Pressure Point" was written just for you! You can make it through this season! Walk in confidence today and take the pressure off!

The challenge for the week: start new habits for personal growth. On your personal calendar, write down individual goals that will bring self-fulfillment and joy!

Reflection Page

Single Until: Challenge/Confirmation/Change

My challenge:

Make a list of things that challenge you in your singleness.

My confirmation for today:

(Start with an *I am* statement.) What is the Lord speaking to you in your singleness right now?

Change:

Write some things you wish you could change in your life while dealing with being single.

Seasons, Reasons, and Lessons

One thing I would pray over this generation of singles is to understand and discern the season that you are in. *"For everything there is a season, and a time for every matter under heaven" (Ecclesiastes 3:1).* I will repeat this over and over again in this passage; you will go through seasons. The things you go through will be for a reason. What you learn in the season is a valuable lesson. Can we just rip the Band-Aid off?

Some people are only in your life for a particular time frame. It may be for a month, ten years, or a couple of weeks. What happens is we hold on to people and situations and stay in a certain place because we are *comfortable*! If you ever find yourself complacent, you can be rest assured that you are not growing. Being stagnant and not growing can only lead to more confusing times for your life. Please, find assurance that there is *more* for your life. Be very careful about the individuals you allow in each season because not only are they bringing themselves, they are bringing a spirit. Check out 1 Thessalonians 5:23. Whatever spirit that person brings for that season will make an impact and influence on your day-to-day life. That is why it is important to understand that *not* everyone will be able to handle the season that you are in. Not everyone can go where the Lord is trying to take you.

Say it again with me; there are seasons you need to recognize and understand before you will ever reach your God-given potential. Everyone on your life team needs to be confident in your God-given dream! Seasons come, and seasons go! You may even find yourself going through something you just went through a couple of years ago. The only way the cycle stops is to recognize the season, reevaluate your habits, and resist the temptation of going back.

I am a huge advocate for growth. If I am not growing in life, then I reevaluate my personal habits. I break up with negative mindsets and place my mind on things above and not on things of the Earth. If I find myself stagnant in my singleness, I recognize the season and discern who has access to my every day. The people in my life, are they helping me or hindering me? Do you continue to take that person back after a breakup? Why is that? Are there some past issues and past hurts that you need to deal with before entering into a relationship? *"He changes times and seasons; he removes kings and sets up kings, he gives wisdom to the wise and knowledge to have understanding" (Daniel 2:21).*

God will give you wisdom (once you pray for wisdom.) Pray for wisdom when considering who you should date, marry, or be friends with. God will grant you with understanding about your current situation and circumstance. You aren't going crazy. You aren't going through a midlife crisis. You are transitioning from one season to the next. Whatever you didn't learn in one season, God will continue to transform you with different situations until you get what He needs to get out of you. What is God teaching you right now? Your strategy for this month should be to focus on what season you are in right now. Who is influencing your life right now? Identify the people who are in your life right now. Are you in the mourning season, the joyous season, or the season of "I don't know?"

The challenge for the week: figure out what God is trying to teach you during this season. Because there is a reason, and there is definitely a lesson that will build your character.

Reflection Page

Single Until: Challenge/Confirmation/Change

My challenge:

Make a list of things that challenge you in your singleness.

My confirmation for today:

(Start with an *I am* statement.) What is the Lord speaking to you in your singleness right now?

Change:

Write some things you wish you could change in your life while dealing with being single.

*Everyone on your life team needs to be
confident in your God-given dream!*

Paid In Full

But love your enemies, do good, and lend,
hoping for nothing in return; and your reward will be great,
and you will be sons of the Most High.

—Luke 6:35

If you are anything like me, you have probably heard or even said, "When prayers go up, blessings come down." You do know that is not an actual scripture, right? However, I do believe that God sends us blessings so that we may bless other people.

Psalm 67 encourages us to praise and thank God. When was the last time that you thanked God that you were single? We have become so self-focused that we have stopped meeting the needs in our communities, workplaces, and even our churches. In this time of waiting, it is crucial that you figure out what you are investing in. Are you investing all your time on throwing pity parties? Are you investing your mental stability into people who don't celebrate you? What has God given you, and how can you meet the needs of the people around you?

Here is the downfall of making the investment into someone that you have taken interest in. You may be spending so much time on that person and doing so much for that individual that you are missing the moment to bless someone else. Let me tell you a little about me and how "don't break the bank" became a part of this devotional.

Growing up, when I got in trouble, when my dad would yell at me after ball games, he would buy me gifts to persuade me that "we were good." My dad was the first man I fell in love with. So this "buying" gifts to make someone like me has actually been a curse rather than a blessing. Don't get me wrong, I love blessing others. I love giving. Please, do not judge me, but I have found myself in situations in which I would try to buy someone's attention and affection through gifts. I can't tell you how much money I have spent on gifts for guys who really didn't even like me. In reality, what I was doing was rejecting the needs of my community. If you find yourself thinking, *Well, if I pay for this, if I spend time with this person, if I do that for that person*, realize that it does *not* mean that the person is going to return or reciprocate at the level that you are on. If your motive is pure, and you hope for nothing in return, your reward will be great. You must check your motive. Why are you spending so much on gifts for that person if you're not dating them? How much time have you spent, trying to get their attention? When referring to investment, I am talking about making a decision to "put all of your eggs in one basket," and "keep your eye on the prize." You see it, you like it, you want it, you buy it type of desire for a person. You will do anything and everything in your power to have this person in your life. You invest spiritually, emotionally, and financially, and prayerfully, it is reciprocated.

I want to encourage you to be mindful of how you invest in the one that you have a crush on. You do *not* have to break the bank to make them know how you feel. I have spent so much on depositing on someone that I was interested in, and now, we have cut ties. I'm *not* saying don't bless people. I am saying, however, if you like someone, make sure that you are not breaking the bank to prove how much you care because it is not worth it, especially if you do not know where they stand with their feelings for you.

In this season of singleness, take a step back. What's your motive for paying for dinner? Why are you always the one sacrificing your time? What are the needs around you right now in your community, school, or at church? How can you make the investment into the needs around you, instead of the person that may not even like you? Please, stop breaking your bank, trying to make someone like you. This may be with so-called "friends" as well. Friendships should be fruitful. Relationships should produce fruit! The person you are interested in should be worth your time, energy, and effort. Isaiah 53:5 should be a reminder that Jesus paid it all. Today be encouraged to do good, lend and hope for nothing in return.

Reflection Page

Single Until: Challenge/Confirmation/Change

My challenge:

Make a list of things that challenge you in your singleness.

My confirmation for today:

(Start with an *I am* statement.) What is the Lord speaking to you in your singleness right now?

Change:

Write some things you wish you could change in your life while dealing with being single.

Blueprint for Marriage

First Corinthians 13:4–13 is a very familiar passage. This scripture is the most popular scripture during weddings. You're right, it is the "love is patient" scripture. There are three words that make a biblical marriage and relationship stand: faith, hope, and love.

I was very apprehensive about writing this section on the "blueprint for marriage." I can see some of you now with your nose turned up in the air. "Who does she think she is, telling us that there is a blueprint for marriage, she has never been married!" You're right, I have never been married! I do believe that our society has commercialized marriage into this billion-dollar industry that ruins the sanity of most individuals. But I believe that God has set me aside for such a time as this to get my generation back to kingdom marriages. One thing I know, the B-I-B-L-E *is* the blueprint for marriage.

Blueprints are made so that we can have a plan. Could you imagine building a house without a plan? The question I have for you right now is who is providing godly marriage counseling in your singleness? I don't want to wait until I am in a relationship, engaged, and then go to counseling for six months before the marriage begins. You want to know who is teaching us and what is preparing this next generation for marriage. Our homes and social media! That's who is teaching us right now!

Social media and reality TV are the most solid foundations right now that will make the most impact. We are the generation, unfortunately, that has no sustainability about us. Longevity is a foreign word. Unfortunately, today's single is self-centered. Right now, we are developing habits and patterns that are either of the world or grounded in the word. You, reading this today, let me say this again;

you are either a single person *in* the *Word* or *of* the *world*. The examples that are in your life right now concerning marriage are making a huge imprint on your future relationships. The way your dad is treating your mom right now is cultivating your perception of the way one should be treated. The way your mom speaks to your dad in this very moment will have an impact on how you speak to your husband! Your normal right now may be that your mom raised you by herself, and you have a fear that could be your reality. We aren't worried about *covenant*, but we are fixated on *contract*. Listen, a *contract* can be broken; a *covenant* cannot! The new covenant encourages us that Jesus made the ultimate sacrifice for us, and what He promised us is ours.

Therefore, your relationship reflects two things. Number one, our relationships with our parents, and secondly, the relationship we have with Christ. One more time, say this out loud, "*My relationship reflects my relationship with Christ!*" So if you are spending five minutes with Jesus, living for Him one day a week, the friendships that you are in are going to reflect that! If you only pray when you get in trouble or are in a desperate situation, how will your prayer life in your relationship reflect that? There must be a plan, a system, or a strategy that is going to help you build on the principles for your marriage.

Thanks to resources at our fingertips, there are podcasts, books, and YouTube sermon series that we need to take advantage of in our singleness! We need to retain information right now that will help us build kingdom marriages. Pastor Jentzen Franklin said this: "Marriage does not make you who you are. It reveals who you are." When I read that, I was convicted, and I am not even married. We must draw a blueprint right now in our singleness that will help us build our future marriages. On the reflection page, take time to draw foundational words that will build up your future marriage. Also, write down some key resources that you are taking advantage of in this time, and share them with a friend! I'll start you off with some keywords for your blueprint: faith, hope, and love!

Reflection Page

Single Until: Challenge/Confirmation/Change

My challenge:

Make a list of things that challenge you in your singleness.

My confirmation for today:

(Start with an *I am* statement.) What is the Lord speaking to you in your singleness right now?

Change:

Write some things you wish you could change in your life while dealing with being single.

*We are developing habits and patterns that are
either of the world or grounded in the word.*

Stop Forcing Things
That Do Not Fit

Can I be honest right now? I am addicted to the game of Tetris. Tetris is a digital block puzzle game, and the ultimate goals is to rotate and drop shaped blocks down on a game board, trying to align them with one another. Your goal is to take the pieces given and make one straight row to eliminate that row. Sounds confusing, I know! However, what I love about this game is that it is a game of strategy! Write this down: "*I need a strategy!*" If the Tetris analogy was confusing, just write the word *strategy* down somewhere close! I would compare it to the board game, Jenga!

I love a good strategy for life. On your jobs, you need a strategy. In your future relationships, you need a game plan. In your singleness, you must have a blueprint for your sanity. Again, in the game, you must rotate and drop certain blocks to fit in the right places. How does this apply to your singleness? Each day, you are trying to figure out where you fit in being single, especially if you have friends who are in relationships. Not only are you trying to find your place but also your purpose.

It is crucial to figure out the who, what, how, and why in your single life. Are you forcing friendships? Are you wearing outfits that get the attention of the opposite sex? Why do you allow your ex to continue to come in and out of your life? Are you making choices based off of your feelings instead of your faith? Why are you feeling frustrated right now? Who can you call when you are discouraged when you see wedding announcements and baby shower invites? Like the blocks of Tetris, are you building a wall in your singleness? You can lose this game easily if you allow the blocks to get to a certain height. Has your heart become hardened? Are you isolating yourself to a point that is unhealthy? Or are you choosing to remove and annihilate toxic thinking and toxic relationships?

This week, I challenge you to draw a picture like the one illustrated here. Obviously, I was just giving you examples of what would be in my boxes. But take some time out this week to navigate through your personal life.

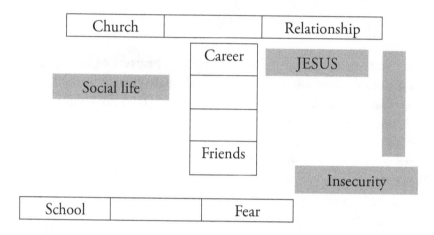

Let's say the above illustration is your life right now. Your challenge this week is to make your own shapes on a piece of paper. Fill in those shapes with words that shape who you are and where you want to be in five years. List things you want to work on and the priorities in your life right now. Frustration enters our life when we continue to force things that are not supposed to be there. It's uncomfortable when the Lord starts removing people to get our attention. It may be uncomfortable right now, but it is necessary for growth when the Lord takes us through the removal process and removes the pieces that we forced into our life.

Today, let our prayer be: Lord, I need a strategy while I am single. I need a plan of action that will help me stay focused on You. Your Word says that You have plans to prosper me and not to harm me. Plans to give me a hope and a future. Who do I need to let go of in this season so that You may bless me with the right things that are needed for my destiny? Lord, reveal to me some places in my life that I am trying to force myself into. Am I forcing myself in relationships because I am afraid to be lonely? Today, God, connect with my heart and help me focus on my relationship with You! In Jesus's name, we do pray. Amen.

Reflection Page

Single Until: Challenge/Confirmation/Change

My challenge:

Make a list of things that challenge you in your singleness.

My confirmation for today:

(Start with an *I am* statement.) What is the Lord speaking to you in your singleness right now?

Change:

Write some things you wish you could change in your life while dealing with being single.

The First

"You shall love the Lord your God with all your heart,
with all your soul, and with all your mind."
This is the first and greatest commandment.
You shall love your neighbor as yourself.
—Matthew 22:37–39

Albert Einstein said, "If you want to live a happy life, tie it to a goal, not to people or things." There is just something about the *"firsts"* in your life. Your *first-time experiences* hold significant value in your memory that influences your day-to-day life. Think about your first car you ever drove; your first crush that began on the monkey bars at the elementary playground; your first kiss; the first person you fell in love with; the first time you rode a bike without training wheels; your first "I love you!" Think about your *first* steps that you ever took as an infant. Can you remember that? Probably not, but I am absolutely sure your parents have some type of video they play on every birthday! You will also remember the first time someone hurt your feelings, or when someone broke your heart into a million pieces. This is for everyone to think about, but the first man that you fall in love with is your dad. Your future relationships are going to be determined by two people—your mother and your father. You can disagree with me. I read once that daughters marry someone just like their dads. And sons marry someone just like their mothers. As twisted as that may seem, I believe it.

For females, the first man that you ever fall in love with is your dad! If the relationship between father and daughter is unstable, fragile, or dysfunctional, somewhere down the line, her future relationships will be the same. I'm not going to leave the guys out. My mom put it this way: "How a guy treats his mother and sisters is how he will treat you!" All I am saying is that our parents play a huge role in our future relationships! So what happens when the first person we fall in love with shatters our dreams, our self-esteem, and self-worth? What if you grew up in an absent-father or absent-mother home?

I believe that we have to heal from those moments. I also believe we owe the person God places in our lives an explanation of what we may struggle with due to our childhood. Unnecessary baggage is just that—unnecessary. I would rather communicate in the early stages of a relationship about all the baggage I am carrying than wait until a breaking point in the relationship where everything is revealed. Everything in the dark always comes to the light. Listen, I come from a two-parent home. I am the apple of my dad's eye, and my mommy's little princess. I am not being boastful at all. Whomever I marry must know that I am who I am because of my parents. My parents raised me to be independent, self-sufficient, determined, and bold.

For forty-seven years, my parents have set the example of what a godly marriage should look like. Was their marriage perfect? Of course not! Did they have disagreements and live paycheck to paycheck? Sure did! Out of their struggle, I learned how to balance a checkbook. Did they argue over the smallest of things? They did and still do to this day! What I do know is they have unconditional love for each other. I am encouraged that I was able to see the struggle but see them submit to the Savior in the good times and the bad. Their marriage served as the first ministry I was ever a part of. They do submit and surrender to Jesus Christ first.

The way I was raised has a huge influence on who I am today and how I love other people. I believe that everything starts in your home. Character is built, core values are determined, discipline is established, work ethic is produced, and your faith is set on course right in the four walls of your own home. I want to emphasize that what is inside of you will eventually come out of you. So it is important for you to ask God to heal what hurts. Not only that, but you have to understand what you are bringing to the table in a relationship. Since my parents struggled with their finances (I never knew, by the way), I decided that wasn't going to be me! I am a penny-pincher, and tithing is important to me! I taught myself how to invest and talk to financial advisors. Why do I tell you all of this? Because I want to encourage you that if you are praying for someone that is financially stable, make sure you are.

When I used the illustration of "I know what I bring to the table," think about it this way: if my table is set with fine china, a guy who wants to settle with eating off of paper plates may not be the one for me. P.S. there isn't anything wrong with paper plates; I eat off them all the time. It was just to make a point. My point is if I am preparing myself right now in my singleness, emotionally, physically, and financially (fine china); and if a guy is broke, doesn't believe in counseling, and has no job (paper plate), he may not be the one for me. Again, I refuse to settle.

My challenge question: what is the first thing that has captured your heart but has distorted your relationship with Jesus Christ? Is He first in your life? The first commandment is to "love the Lord your God with all of your heart, soul, and mind. The second commandment is to "love your neighbor as yourself."

I want to encourage you this week to make a list of things you put *first* before God. I want to challenge you to love God, love yourself, and to love others. Today, take the first step into realizing that God wants to heal you and to make you whole. People may disappoint you, but God never will! What have you tied your happiness to? Is the person you are with right now your top priority? Is your job, school, money, or your own happiness first in your life? God is concerned about our happiness, but He is more concerned with our holiness. Let's make Jesus the first person we talk to this week. The first person we cry out to. The first person to catch us if we fall this week! Make Jesus the first in your life, and I promise everything else will come. Matthew 6:33 makes this true. If we seek first the kingdom of God, all the rest will be added unto us.

Reflection Page

Single Until: Challenge/Confirmation/Change

My challenge:

Make a list of things that challenge you in your singleness.

My confirmation for today:

(Start with an *I am* statement.) What is the Lord speaking to you in your singleness right now?

Change:

Write some things you wish you could change in your life while dealing with being single.

Weak *Flesh*, Strong *Faith*

The acts of the flesh are obvious: sexual immorality, impurity,
and debauchery; idolatry and witchcraft; hatred, discord, jealousy,
fits of rage, selfish ambition, dissensions, factions, and envy;
drunkenness, orgies, and the lie. I warn you, as I did before,
that those who live like this will not inherit the kingdom of God.
—Galatians 5:19–21

Have you ever found yourself saying, "But everyone is doing it?"

Then, your mom would say, "If everyone jumps off a bridge, would you?"

Jokingly you say in that moment, "*Yes*, because everyone is doing it!"

Let's talk about our *flesh* for just one moment!

"Watch and pray, that ye enter not into temptation: the spirit is willing, but the *flesh* is weak" (Matthew 26:41).

Works of the Flesh

"The spirit is willing, but the flesh is weak" *(Matthew 26:41)*.
"Explains the *works* of the *flesh*" *(Galatians 5:19–21)*.

1. Sexual immorality
2. Impurity
3. Jealousy
4. Selfish ambition
5. Drunkenness

You get it right? We must understand that God calls us to be sober-minded in our friendships and relationships that we are in right now! Why does the Lord call us to set our minds on things that are above and not on things of the Earth? Because the enemy prowls around like a roaring lion, seeking someone to devour! *Future reading: Colossians 3:23 and 1 Peter 5:8.*

Just because it's not the norm to wait to have sex until marriage, why not be the one that takes a stand? More and more people are finding themselves in difficult situations because of an instant impulse they made from their flesh! Generational curses can be broken, and generational wealth can be obtained when being in right standing with God. We say today, "I just got caught up in the moment." Well, that moment is a moment that you will never get back! In that one moment, you compromised your ministry. In that one moment, the enemy was able to get you out of character, and you find yourself further and further away from Christ! I get teased all the time about waiting to have sex until marriage! I am not going to allow my flesh to win! I refuse to take advantage of God's grace.

How do you know if you are taking advantage of grace? When you allow your flesh to win! If you have the mentality of "Well, God is going to forgive me anyway!" Our flesh is weak. We need conviction from the holy spirit to guide us through the under pressure moments. From the scripture reading above, what fleshly desires are you dealing with today? Write them down and repent! Repentance is just turning away from those things that hinder your relationship with Christ. Ask God to strengthen your faith. Stop feeding your flesh.

Reflection Page

Single Until: Challenge/Confirmation/Change

My challenge:

Make a list of things that challenge you in your singleness.

My confirmation for today:

(Start with an *I am* statement.) What is the Lord speaking to you in your singleness right now?

Change:

Write some things you wish you could change in your life while dealing with being single.

You are either waiting in expectation or you are in contemplation. There is a difference between seeing and looking!

The Assignment Carrier

This may be the deal breaker of the day! This is one of those pages you will read and possibly cringe after reading. This is a strategy I just need you to understand and try to implement when you desire to date, *talk* to, take interest in, or *court*. (Who uses that word anymore?) This strategy is to be used if you see that person in your life for a very long time in your future. As you all know, we live in a swipe left or right society. It's all about choices. The choices we make today will make a huge impact on our tomorrow. If you're wanting to pursue, date, or make the emotional investment in a person, I want you to ask yourself one question: can they carry the assignment that God has placed on *your* life? And vice versa, can you carry the assignment that God has placed on *their* life?

Some of you are asking what is an "assignment" from God? This is not just a cliché word that we lightly use in church. I believe in assignments, callings, purpose, and vision with my whole entire heart! I believe that you—yes, you—have an assignment from Jesus that only you can fulfill. Think about Noah who had an assignment of building the ark. How about David whose assignment was to kill Goliath. God gave Joshua specific instructions for his task at hand when it came to the Jericho wall. The person that you are spending the most time with should have a "first seat" into what God has called you to do. Even though you may be physically attracted to them, emotionally connected to them, and you may have amazing chemistry, I want you to ask yourself, "Are they ready to tackle the ministry assignment that God has given to me?" I get it; some of you are like, "I'm not in ministry..." Oh, sweetie, but you are! Everything that you are involved in right now is ministering to someone! If the Lord calls you to host a Bible study in your dorm room, would the person you are dating be okay with that? *"Walk with the wise and become wise, for a companion of fools suffers harm" (Proverbs 13:20).* Think about it this way; if a teacher gives you an assignment in Monday, sets a date for you to turn it in by Friday, and says you can pick a partner to work with, would you choose a partner who just wanted *you* to do all the work by yourself? I hope not!

Assignment carriers help you get the task done! You want the *right* person to invest in those areas of your life! The right people are called "assignment carriers." They keep you accountable, help you reach your highest potential, and they want to see you succeed in life. The "assignment carries" make sure you are hitting the mark on your Christian journey! In the book of Genesis, we are directed to the word *helpmeet* or *helpmate*. A helpmate is someone that is there to *help* you!

Single(s), let's just keep it real for a moment. Whatever God has called you to do—big or small—He has prearranged the who, the what, and the where. *"I, Paul, am on special assignment for Christ, carrying out God's plan laid out in the message of life by Jesus" (2 Timothy 1:1–2).* The last relationship didn't work out for a reason. God removed that toxic person from your life because they were a distraction for your growth. Being connected to the right sources will help you with your elevation process. At this moment, we are talking about choosing a companion that may be able to help you and work with you on whatever the Lord has placed before you. Let me ask again. Can the person that you are with carry the assignment that God has placed before you? Just like a teacher, what assignment has God given you to grow His kingdom?

Reflection Page

Single Until: Challenge/Confirmation/Change

My challenge:

Make a list of things that challenge you in your singleness.

My confirmation for today:

(Start with an *I am* statement.) What is the Lord speaking to you in your singleness right now?

Change:

Write some things you wish you could change in your life while dealing with being single.

God can use who He wants, when He wants, for how He wants whenever He wants.

No Fear—All Faith

Look! He has placed the land in front of you.
Go! And occupy it as the Lord, the God of your ancestors, has
promised you! Don't be afraid! Don't be discouraged!
—Deuteronomy 1:21

I ask myself this every morning: "Will my future self appreciate what I am doing today?" If the answer is no, then I find a way to create a new way to think. The goal for the day is to set my future self up for greatness! What does this have to do with your future relationships or your singleness? *Everything!* Right now, wherever you are in life, you are setting your future self up to either fail or succeed. You have heard it before; you are either feeding your faith, or you are feeding your fear.

Max Lucado said it best, "Feed your fears, and your faith will starve. Feed your faith, your fear will." We must starve our fears in this season of being single. Are you setting yourself up to succeed financially, spiritually, and emotionally? Are you praying that your future partner will be financially, spiritually, and emotionally stable? Make sure you are making strides to be that as well! You have the power to create the very person God has designed for you to be. What gets in your way of success? What gets in your way of your relationship with Christ? There is only *one* thing—*you*! If you keep talking yourself out of everything, if you continue to tell yourself that you can't do it, you might as well give up. It is time to push pause on your whole life when you find yourself getting in the way of God's plan. If your insecurities are speaking louder in this season than they ever have, it is time to get back in the Word of God.

This is my lane. This is my purpose and my passion. I love speaking life into people who want to quit and want to give up. Right now, in your singleness, this is not the time to quit or give up on God. This is the time to redefine and refocus your energy. Please meditate on Deuteronomy 1:21. You just read about assignments; let's talk about land! Let's figure out what Deuteronomy 1:21 has to do with your life and your singleness! Prayerfully, what you are about to read will open your eyes in the season that you are in! We can all agree, at one point or the other, we have found ourselves in an emotional place in our singleness! While single, you may have even experienced being in a negative head space in which you couldn't stop overthinking every little detail of life. Have you ever been there? Do not become so distracted on what you don't have that you miss what you do have in this season of your singleness! Hopefully you have a community that is supporting you. Prayerfully you have peace that is surpassing all understanding. What do you have in this season?

He has placed the land in front of you (Deuteronomy 1:21). What land has God placed in front of you? Is it mentoring younger people, attending nursing school, encouraging your teammates, missions, full-time ministry, or volunteering? There are people right now that need your story and need to hear your testimony. How are you making it in your singleness? What has God taught you and promised you in the days to come? "Occupy the land." Work with what you have, where you are at! There are other singles that need you, there are people on your job who are discouraged, and there are people at your school that need to know how you are making it! Remember this in your singleness, "There are different *resources* that God will provide through different *relationships*" (anonymous). There is no time for fear! This week, right down your fears! After you right down your fears, take a moment and feed your faith through the Word of God.

Reflection Page

Single Until: Challenge/Confirmation/Change

My challenge:

Make a list of things that challenge you in your singleness.

My confirmation for today:

(Start with an *I am* statement.) What is the Lord speaking to you in your singleness right now?

Change:

Write some things you wish you could change in your life while dealing with being single.

Distractions will always delay your destiny.

Wrong Number, God!

Each of you should use whatever gift you have received to serve others, as faithful stewards of God's grace in its various forms.
—1 Peter 4:10

Single, married, divorced, widowed, single again, or called to be single, this is for you! I am certain of one thing—that nothing great ever comes from comfort zones! Pastor Sheryl Brady is one of my favorite pastors of all times. She said, "If you can't appreciate your struggle, you will never appreciate your season." Write that down on a Post-it note! Maybe you are struggling right now in your singleness. Maybe #thestruggleisreal, but can I tell you, so is your God!

Venting on social media is a pet peeve of mine. Everyone has an opinion these days. Instead of attacking the problem like we were taught in middle school, we definitely attack the person with a subliminal message. What I absolutely love about my cell phone is that I have two options. I can accept or decline the call. The other thing I love about my cell phone is that whoever is calling me, their number shows up and their name too, so I know who it is. My close contacts have a picture with their number, which means that they are in my inner circle!

Here, recently, the contact that has continued to call is "spam risk." When "spam risk" calls, I have two options to accept or ignore. When I press the ignore button, it directly goes straight to voicemail. Which has my prerecorded voice asking them to leave a brief message. Can I tell you that God is getting tired of us pressing ignore in our lives? He is tired of declining the call that is on our life. We treat God like He is "spam risk." When we ignore the call for our life, God has the authority to start looking for someone who will answer. Rest assured that God has called you to something great while in your singleness. You have the option to either accept or ignore His call in this time. "For we are His workmanship, created in Christ Jesus for good works, which God prepared beforehand that we should walk in them" (Ephesians 2:10).

Whatever assignment the Lord has designed for you in this specific season, it is to help you recognize the gifts and talents He has placed within you. Some of you haven't even tapped into the potential of what God has placed inside of you yet! Don't allow your singleness to prevent you from serving with excellence! What do I mean? I have had people tell me that I couldn't work at their church because I wasn't married! Just because you are "doing" life right now by yourself does not mean that you have to decline God's call. *Say this out loud: God is calling me!* Believe that God has plans to proper you and not to harm you! Please understand this; people's assumption concerning you will never stop the calling God has for you! What does that mean? Let's say you had a really bad breakup or that a friendship/relationship didn't work out the way you wanted it to. That does not mean that life stops! Let's say people assume that you are an extreme introvert. Never allow the expectations of a person derail you from who God has called you to be! If people are talking about you, if people are making fun of you because you're single, and you're always hanging out with couples, it really is okay!

In the next couple of days, allow God to love on you! Figure out what you are good at! Go serve your community, job, and your church with excellence! Stir up the gifts that are inside of you today! And celebrate that you are created in Christ Jesus for good works! God doesn't have the wrong number! He knew who He was calling when He called you! Are you going to answer?

Reflection Page

Single Until: Challenge/Confirmation/Change

My challenge:

Make a list of things that challenge you in your singleness.

My confirmation for today:

(Start with an *I am* statement.) What is the Lord speaking to you in your singleness right now?

Change:

Write some things you wish you could change in your life while dealing with being single.

Developing Negatives

And have put on the new self, which is being renewed
in knowledge after the image of its creator.

—Colossians 3:10

Before I received my cell phone, I used to love to take pictures with a disposable camera. I would save up my money just to buy the cameras at the local drugstores in my hometown. This was way before selfies and using filters to cover up flaws. Disposable cameras are unique because there is a limit on how many pictures you could take. Not only that, but you have to turn the camera back in to the drugstore so that the negatives could develop. Today, I Google searched how to develop negatives. Here are the facts when developing negatives while using a disposal camera.

Facts:

1. Take your negatives to a photo lab or drugstore
2. Enlarge your negatives optically in a darkroom using an enlarger
3. Negatives are usually formed on transparent material
4. Exposure—projecting the negative image onto paper, reverses the tones, and produces a positive photographic print.

Please, stay with me! I believe a strategy in your success in your single season is to "develop your negatives." Just like a disposable camera, the first fact is to take our negatives to Jesus and place them right at His feet. Ephesians 4:24 says that we must "put on our new self, created after the likeness of God in true righteousness and holiness." Once we take our "negatives" or our patterns that do not reflect God and place them at His feet, He will begin to enlarge our negatives. I don't know about you, but I would rather for God to enlarge my negatives in the secret place of His hands then have Him expose me in front of other people.

If you are reading this right now, God wants your anger. God wants your broken pieces. God wants your pride. God wants your jealousy. God wants your lustful thoughts. Right now, if you are dealing with those negatives, you are in the darkroom. I want to encourage you that God has called you in to His marvelous light. What we must understand while we are single is transparency will always reveal truth, and truth will always set us free.

I mentioned before that when taking a picture with a disposable camera, there aren't any filters you get to choose to make your picture seem perfect. Being transparent with others when you struggle is not a weakness. Allowing God to transform you while being transparent will ultimately develop you mentally, physically, and spiritually. The last fact of how to develop negatives is exposure. Exodus 20:1–26 says, "And God spoke all these words, saying, 'I am the Lord your God, who brought you out of the land of Egypt, out of the house of bondage. You shall have no other gods before me. You shall not make for yourself a carved image, or any likeness of anything that is in heaven above, or that is in the earth beneath, or that is in the water under the earth. You shall not bow down to them or serve them, for I the Lord your God am a jealous God.'"

I believe God exposes our true nature under pressure. I believe that we are exposed in times of adversity. I believe that as you are walking through this process of being single, God is establishing who He is in your life. We don't get to use a filter to mask what we are going through in our singleness. Infatuation with a person can become your god. Lust can consume your heart, and you can find yourself "bowing down" to lust because you feel as though it is healthier than actually creating a physical act. This is the perfect time to "develop your negatives." This week, ask God to reveal and expose your negatives to you. Allow God to reverse the tones of your life and produce what will ultimately project the picture of God and His righteousness and holiness in and through your life.

Reflection Page

Single Until: Challenge/Confirmation/Change

My challenge:

Make a list of things that challenge you in your singleness.

My confirmation for today:

(Start with an *I am* statement.) What is the Lord speaking to you in your singleness right now?

Change:

Write some things you wish you could change in your life while dealing with being single.

Transparency will always reveal the truth
and truth will always set you free.

Version 2.0

Have you ever found yourself buying the newest and next best version of your cell phone? It doesn't matter if you are team iPhone or team android; whenever a new version comes out, you are attracted to the *newest* features for that phone. We must admire the phone companies for making each version better than the last. Your challenge while reading is to figure out how to make a better version of yourself while single!

Version is defined as *a particular form of something differing in certain respects from an earlier form or other forms of the same type of thing.* What does this have to do with you and your singleness? Right now, while in your singleness, you have the capability of becoming the best version of yourself. That last breakup did *not* break you! The last relationship that you were in did *not* put a halt on where God wants to take you or what He wants to do through you. Maybe you have never dated someone seriously. God has not forgotten about you. This is the time to figure out your bad habits, tap into your moral compass, and recreate or redefine a better version of yourself.

A version 2.0 of you is necessary for success in your singleness. Look at your phone right now. Every so often, a notification will come up and ask you to update your phone. One of the worst things you can do right now is not push the update button on your life. I am not saying you have to update your wardrobe or your physical appearance. However, I am saying that you should update your mindset, your skill set, and your basic fundamentals of communication while in this season. Read Genesis 16:1–16. If you are into reality TV, this is the show to watch in Genesis 16:1, "Sarai, Abram's wife hadn't yet produced a child. Sarai said to Abram, 'God has not seen fit to let me have a child. Sleep with my maid. Maybe I can get a family from her.'"

Can we just push pause for a second! This woman of God, Sarah, told her *husband* to sleep with their *maid*! Some of you are probably rolling your eyes. But think about it this way: some of us in our singleness have been in that desperate moment where we date for convenience, we compromise our standards, or like Sarah, we begin to doubt God and take matters into our own hands. If we place ourselves in Sarah's shoes, instead of laughing *at* God, we need to *trust* God and *trust* God's timing! Sarah found herself making decisions ahead of God. While in your singleness, I pray that you take this time to create a better version of yourself. This is not the time to get ahead of God, laugh at God, or think that God has forgotten about you!

Your goal for this week is to *recreate* a 2.0 version of yourself and push yourself to update your personal interactions with other people. First thing to start with is your heart. Second thing is to put down your actual phone and have a conversation with someone face-to-face.

The 2.0 version of yourself should be *better* than the old you! The 2.0 version of yourself should not settle! The 2.0 version of yourself should become the best version of yourself while you are by yourself. *Version* 2.0 starts today!

Reflection Page

Single Until: Challenge/Confirmation/Change

My challenge:

Make a list of things that challenge you in your singleness.

My confirmation for today:

(Start with an *I am* statement.) What is the Lord speaking to you in your singleness right now?

Change:

Write some things you wish you could change in your life while dealing with being single.

Trust God and Trust God's timing.

"Seed, Need, Feed"

You have heard it said before, "Your attitude determines your altitude" (2 Timothy MSG). Attitude is everything. It affects everything and everyone around you. Your attitude is going to determine whether you stay in the season that you are in or how quick you get out of that particular season. Right now, in your singleness, your *attitude* is a determining fact of if you are ready for a relationship or not.

"Now the parable is this the seed is the word of God" (Luke 8:11).

Seed. Be careful in this season with what attitude seed you are planting in your life. How is my attitude while I am waiting on God? Are you the type of person that is pouting when you should be praising? Are you worrying when you could be worshiping? Right now, are you walking in bitterness, or do you know how blessed you are? The seed is the Word of God! Has your attitude hindered your pursuit of your relationship with Christ? In Philippians 1:27, Paul writes, "Whatever happens, conduct yourselves in a manner worthy of the gospel of Christ." Right now, you could be frustrated in your singleness. Maybe you are dealing with unexpected distractions that have you questioning if God has someone for you. Wherever you may find yourself right now, please understand that how you respond in the situation should reflect the attitude of Jesus Christ. The attitude of Christ even in His season of waiting was that of pleasing His Father. Christ's attitude was of patience during discouragement. His attitude was kind in the midst of hostility. His attitude is one of love. Those are the seeds that we should gravitate toward in this season. The seeds of love. The seeds of peace. The seeds of joy.

"To put off your old self, which belongs to your former manner of life and is corrupt through deceitful desires, and to be renewed in the

spirit of your minds, and to put on the new self, created after the likeness of God in true righteousness and holiness" (Ephesians 4:22–24 ESV).

Need. Not only is God checking our attitude while we are waiting, but God is also checking our attitude when we are writing the vision for our life. I am not saying that we shouldn't have four hundred different Pinterest boards; however, if that vision is taken away from the vision that God has for your life, we need to check our hearts and check our attitudes. "Write the vision, and make it plain, yet the vision is yet for the appointed time" (Habakkuk 2:2). Wait for it! We need to establish what seeds we are planting while still single. What does God value? What vision has God given you?

Feed. Micah 7:7 is a friendly reminder that as we wait and as we check our attitude, God hears us! "But as for me, I will look unto God; I will wait for the God of my salvation: My God will hear me." Please be careful that as you are waiting on God, bitterness and jealousy do not take root deep inside of your heart. Does God need to check your attitude? Has your life circumstances created an atmosphere in which your attitude is not a reflection of God's promises? Today, take a deep breath and reflect on what type of atmosphere you are in, but also consider what you are feeding your spirit. Your response in your current situation is reflecting your personal relationship with Jesus Christ.

Challenge for the day: examine your heart! Does my attitude reflect Christ, or do I need an attitude adjustment! Is this a strategy that helps me move forward?

Affirmation: today, my attitude will reflect that of Christ! I can be happy for others! I can serve others with excellence. I am a willing vessel of Jesus Christ! Today, my heart has been examined, and God has created in me a right spirit! Whatever is inside of me will eventually come out of me! God, grab everything out of me that does not bring glory to You!

Reflection Page

Single Until: Challenge/Confirmation/Change

My challenge:

Make a list of things that challenge you in your singleness.

My confirmation for today:

(Start with an *I am* statement.) What is the Lord speaking to you in your singleness right now?

Change:

Write some things you wish you could change in your life while dealing with being single.

Unnecessary baggage hinders our potential, paralyzes our positions, holds us back from what God has for us.

Relationships should always reflect the love of Christ.
Whatever is inside of you will eventually come out of you.

While You Are Waiting

*I remain confident of this: I will see the goodness of the
Lord in the land of the living. Wait for the Lord; be strong,
and let your heart take courage; wait for the Lord!*
—Psalm 27:13–14

Singleness is not designed to make you feel defeated. Oftentimes, the enemy will use your singleness to divert you into thinking that you are not good enough, you're not attractive, no one wants you, or—the worse lie ever—"You are going to be single for the rest of your life." You begin to believe these lies, of course, because of the relationships that you see around you. Instead of focusing on God, you start questioning why God is making you wait! You also begin to believe that God is mad at you! You must be cursed! Maybe those chain letters in middle school that you didn't send to seven people (maybe you should have)! Questions like "What if God really doesn't have someone for me?" or worse yet "What if I'm single for the rest of my life?" fill your mind and then enter your heart. Some of your hearts just dropped into your heart, didn't it! Breathe! Sometimes, while you are waiting, you get overwhelmed and discouraged.

Being frustrated and faithful can leave you exhausted, at times. Maybe you are feeling hopeless instead of being hopeful in your singleness right now. Maybe you have no confidence in seeing the good because your waiting is really weighing you down!

Think about it this way:

Dumbbells come in all different sizes and shapes and weight measurements. You have a variation of dumbbells; ten-pound dumbbells to fifty pounds. Now, depending on your age, body weight, and height, that will determine which type of dumbbell you will use. Stay with me here. Let's take it even further. *Open your spiritual eyes right now.*

The five-pound dumbbell represents lust (let's say you lust after someone who is married, you lust after the things of your flesh). And you continue to pick up this five-pound dumbbell of lust because it's the easiest. You're comfortable with it, and as long as you're building muscle, you're okay with it! The ten-pound dumbbell represents compromise. You compromise on a Friday night because you don't know your worth. You're committed to Christ on Sundays but compromise every other day of the week! All because your flesh is weak. The twenty-pound dumbbell represents believing the lies of the enemy. We pick these dumbbells up every single day! We literally stand in front of the mirror with this dumbbell of lies and speak negatively over everything that is not going right in our life. We allow the enemy to plant seeds of negativity, and it has become a thing of repetition to speak death instead of life over our situations.

While you are waiting in your singleness, the weight you choose to exercise with daily will determine how *fit* you will become while you are waiting. Many of us pick up the twenty-pound weight of lies, the lust weight, and the weight of compromise because, again, our flesh is weak! Choosing the wrong spiritual "weights" while you are single will keep you *un-FIT.*

F—Far from Christ

I—Isolated from doing what God has called you to do

T—Timid in pursing your purpose

When the *waiting* process gets frustrating or overwhelming, remember that you can only become strong through Jesus Christ! The strategy is to identify which weight you are exercising with while you are waiting. Name some of other spiritual weights that you pick up on a daily basis. Reflect on scripture this week and pray that God will open up other areas in your life that may be *un-FIT.* Are you *far* from Christ, *isolated,* and *timid?* Remain confident in knowing that you will see the goodness of Jesus while you wait.

Reflection Page

Single Until: Challenge/Confirmation/Change

My challenge:

Make a list of things that challenge you in your singleness.

My confirmation for today:

(Start with an *I am* statement.) What is the Lord speaking to you in your singleness right now?

Change:

Write some things you wish you could change in your life while dealing with being single.

Vulnerability, Virginity, Validation

The *V* word scares me! For some of you right now, you are trying to figure out every *V* word that is actually terrifying! It's not what you think, so calm down! The *V* words that I will discuss in the next few pages are: vulnerability, virginity, and validation!

Vulnerability

I hate to admit it, but I hate being *vulnerable*! For the longest time in my life, I had to put on this façade of being "tough." If you grew up around my father, you would know why! There was no crying around him! If I was hurt on the playground, there was no running to my parents to kiss the little scrape on my knee! If I was hurt in a sport, my dad would say, "You will be just fine!" If I was picked on, the conversation started, "You better learn how to stick up for yourself." Even with my mother, she would literally wipe the tears, pat me on my behind, and I would be on my way! So I developed this pattern of holding back tears and dismissing when my feelings were hurt, especially if it was in front of people. Why am I telling you all of this? Possibly because I want to be free. If you're reading this, it is okay to let your guard down. God wants to heal those places that are hidden. But make sure your guard is up when it comes to your heart!

The Word of God says, "Above all else, guard your heart." It is one thing to guard your heart, but if you have a barbwire fence around your heart, you may want to check your heart! Can you be honest in this moment as you are reading this? How are you guarding your heart? Have you become numb to guarding your heart? Why are we supposed to guard our hearts? Again, we guard our hearts because it is the well spring of life! Whatever is in you will eventually come out of you! For the millennial reading this, everything is *not* about you! For some of you, maybe you don't struggle with being vulnerable! Maybe you're an open book! You cry at the drop of a hat, wear your heart on your sleeve, and you communicate effectively. Great! Just don't read this section! But if you're anything like me, I suppress the "I feel" statements. I don't think you should hold in how you are feeling. I love when people say what they mean and mean what they say. I love when people are just real and honest with me! No gray areas! You like someone, just tell them; you don't like someone, just tell them! That's my mentality.

However, I know everyone is not like that. Being transparent and vulnerable is the most important thing when it comes to our relationship with God! In Matthew 6:6 in the MSG it says, "Here's what I want you do: Find a quiet, secluded place so you won't be tempted to role play before God." I really want you to be honest with yourself. Have you been role playing before God? Is it hard for you to be vulnerable in your quiet time or even in a corporate worship setting? If you are role playing before God, there is no doubt that you will role play in your future relationships. I heard this statement before: "Everything is magnified in marriage!" If I ever want to have a healthy relationship, I must be able to communicate effectively.

Vulnerability may be the largest baggage that I carry into a relationship. Who doesn't have baggage in their life? Whether it's from past relationships or present struggles, everyone has baggage. Oftentimes, we carry unnecessary baggage into our future, which then hinders our potential, paralyzes our positions, and holds us back from what God has for us. Your baggage blocks your blessing. Today, I want to challenge you with finding a secluded and quiet place! No social media, no placing filters on your faith. Tell God your fears and your dreams! And today, pray for your future spouse, that they may have the patience of being sensitive to your most vulnerable needs!

Reflection Page

Single Until: Challenge/Confirmation/Change

My challenge:

Make a list of things that challenge you in your singleness.

My confirmation for today:

(Start with an *I am* statement.) What is the Lord speaking to you in your singleness right now?

Change:

Write some things you wish you could change in your life while dealing with being single.

Virginity

A majority of you who are reading this devotional know my story! Some of you purchased this devotional because you wanted to support me, and I am forever grateful! Keep in mind, my goal is to reach this next generation. But for the new people reading, take a deep breath because I am about to drop a huge bomb in your life! I am a thirty-two-year-old virgin (gasp). I've shared my testimony with a lot of younger students, and every time I get to that point, they all have this weird look on their face and then awkwardly clap! For my younger audience reading this, your sexual experience defines the conceptualizations of your future sexual behaviors. What does that mean? If you are having sex right now, watching porn right now, addicted to having multiple partners, it is going to affect your future relationship in some way!

For some of you, your story is totally different, and that's okay! Some of you have had multiple partners. I have had many friends laugh at me and call me names because I am waiting! Honestly, it doesn't hurt my feelings one bit. I do feel sorry for those that feel as though they have to give their bodies to someone else to fill a void in their life. Many teenage girls ask me this question: how did you make this decision to wait?

I was fourteen years old, and I remember going to a benefit concert at my high school. I believe Fellowship of Christian Athletes was sponsoring this concert, and I remember the artist gave her testimony. I vaguely remember what she said before she said these words: "I was fifteen when I made a decision that I wanted to honor God with my body! I wanted to wait to have sex until I was married." After that, the decision was easy for me! I wanted to be just like this artist! I believe that God will send you what you need and who you need when you need it! I remember the artist sharing the rest of her testimony, and at the age of twenty-five, God blessed her with her future husband, and the rest was history! Now, although I am still waiting, I am okay with being on the front line for this next generation. We have females in 2019 proposing to guys. We have people who are dealing with their sexual orientation and committing suicide because of it!

We have a generation that is in the experimental stage with relationships. This generation expresses freely how fluid they are all because they want to be accepted and desired! Some are dealing with "daddy issues," and because your father wasn't there, you have slept with multiple people all because of your hurt! I am beyond blessed to say that I had people in my corner that made the same decision that night. I had friends that kept me accountable all through middle school and high school, and it made a huge difference. I had to wait because I wanted to break a generational curse that runs deep in my family line!

Making the decision to not have sex before marriage isn't for the faint at heart. You have to "check your flesh" on multiple occasions. Not only that, but you have to guard your eye gate (what you watch) and guard your ear gate (what you are listening to). People can think that it is abnormal to be in my thirties and be a virgin. Let them think what they want! If I have to be the one to tell this next generation that they are *worth the wait*, so be it! I am waiting for my future husband because I want to honor God with my body. So dear fourteen-year-old who may be reading this, this is just for you. People are going to make fun of you because you are not sexually active. They will call you names, not believe you, and you may even be dismissed on dates because you won't have sex! God is going to honor your waiting process! You may make this decision to release generational blessing in your life. Just because the world says it's okay doesn't mean it's okay! The Word of God says, "Do not conform to the pattern of this world but be transformed by the renewing of your mind" (Romans 12:2). The pattern of this world is to please people. The pattern of the *Word* tells you to "go against the grain." In other words, be different! There is strength in waiting! Pray this today: "God give me the strength while I wait!"

Reflection Page

Single Until: Challenge/Confirmation/Change

My challenge:

Make a list of things that challenge you in your singleness.

My confirmation for today:

(Start with an *I am* statement.) What is the Lord speaking to you in your singleness right now?

Change:

Write some things you wish you could change in your life while dealing with being single.

God will send you what you need,
and who you need when you need it.
This is called a divine alignment.

Validation

If you are single like me and have a hard time being vulnerable like me, listen; this whole "*V*" section is for you! Not only do I struggle with being vulnerable, I also feel as though people have a hard time with vulnerability because we have issues of wanting to be *validated* by other people! Validation for females is a little bit different than males. If we are honest, we are addicted to how many likes we get on social media. We want people to see our post, and the more likes we get, the more validated we feel! We hide behind filters and social media because our value is wrapped up in a package of perfection. The problem is that if we show our true selves, we may have to deal with rejection. The reality is if I have no validation from other people, then I'm really not worth anyone's time. That is a lie from the enemy himself. You are worth it! *Rejection is the thief of confidence.* In Psalm 26, it says: "Vindicate me, O Lord, for I have walked in my integrity, and I have trusted in the Lord without wavering. Examine me, O Lord, and try me; test my mind and my heart. For Your lovingkindness is before my eyes, and I have walked in Your truth."

There are a couple of questions I want to ask you. Whose truth are you walking in right now? Our insecurities scream loud on a day-to-day basis when we do not know what God says about us. Now, you may never be someone's MCM (man crush Monday) or someone's WCW (woman crush Wednesday), but you can say that a man died just for you over two thousand years ago. You can say that you were the first thing on His mind when He died and rose again! Who else would lay down their life just for you?

There is victory once you sacrifice the satisfaction of being validated by people. Are you walking in integrity in this season of singleness? What websites are you clicking on when no one is watching? If you are not being held accountable, what happens when the door is shut on a Friday night? Being validated by Jesus is the approval that is needed for relational growth. "Do not love the world or the things in the world. If anyone loves the world, the love of the Father is not in him" (1 John 2:15).

During this season of singleness, becoming the woman/man God wants you to become depends on a couple of things. First things first, who do you seek validation from? Is it your boyfriend or girlfriend? Do you look for approval from your friends, parents, or teachers? Are you addicted to the *likes* you get from social media? Is there a feeling of security that you feel when you are approved by someone? Security in your singleness can only be satisfied when you are walking in truth. If the Lord were to place you in front of a class and place a light on your heart and your mind to illuminate it, what would the class be able to see if your thoughts and last words spoken were projected for people to see?

Reflect on: Romans 12:11, "Give your bodies as living sacrifices." What's a sacrifice? Something you surrender to God as an offering! Sometimes, you have to tell your flesh no! There is victory once you sacrifice the very thing God wants you to give up!

Reflection Page

Single Until: Challenge/Confirmation/Change

My challenge:

Make a list of things that challenge you in your singleness.

My confirmation for today:

(Start with an *I am* statement.) What is the Lord speaking to you in your singleness right now?

Change:

Write some things you wish you could change in your life while dealing with being single.

Captive Challenge

Demolish arguments and every pretension that sets itself
up against the knowledge of God, and we take captive
every thought to make it obedient to Christ.

—2 Corinthians 10:5

Are you ready to be challenged? Who doesn't like to be challenged? For some, you will read right through this and put a check mark that you read some scripture today! Push pause on this challenge today! Today, I want to challenge you with taking every proudful, boastful, and false thought and *make it* obedient to Christ! Will you underline *make it*! We must understand that in 2 Corinthians 10:5, Paul was trying to destroy arguments and opinions against God. Paul was encouraging everyone to have the mind of Christ. Not only that, but also demolishing worldviews of how we think about Christ in our personal walks.

The goal in our singleness is to destroy any thought that does not line up to God's Word, God's will, or God's way. Our thoughts, our viewpoints of the world, even our ideas should be submitted under the authority of Jesus Christ. Personally, I feel like we have twenty tabs open like a computer in our mind. Our spiritual search engine is always seeking answers in life. There is a competition between positive and negative thoughts, good and bad thoughts, and depending on what "tab" is open in your mind, that will determine the choice you will make for that day or the course of your singleness.

Your wholeness all depends on how you talk to yourself! Do you want to be whole? Do you want to feel complete? It's time to close the tabs of your mind. What you cannot do while single is continue to repeat negative thoughts toward yourself or your singleness. You may be in a valley of negativity but find a way to get out. Do not get stuck in the pit of negative thoughts. There is no way you are going to be able to have a healthy relationship if you are feeding your spirit with negativity all the time! Change your language and the pattern on how you speak to yourself and to others. You've heard the saying before that hurt people hurt people! Now, I'm not saying that your relationship is going to be perfect! However, if you are hurting right now, and you hold that in, it is going to magnify and disguise itself some way and somehow in your future relationships! If you find yourself talking negative to yourself on a Friday night because all of your friends are on dates, take that thought hostage! "Well, no one likes me. I'm not good enough, I'm not smart enough, I'm going to be single forever!" Take those thoughts hostage! Not only take them hostage but *make* your thoughts obedient to Christ! Earlier, I told you to underline *make it*!

This what I want you to do on the reflection page: I want you to write every negative thought you have *ever* had about yourself. After you write a couple of things down, I want you to cross it out and *make it* obedient to Christ! Who does God say that you are? What does God say about your current situation? Think about it this way; *you* are in charge of your thoughts! The Scripture says that we have the power to *demolish* and *take captive*. Those are action words we must consider when it comes to our mind! If your thoughts don't line up to what God says, start *making* your thoughts obedient to Christ!

Reflection Page

Single Until: Challenge/Confirmation/Change

My challenge:

Make a list of things that challenge you in your singleness.

My confirmation for today:

(Start with an *I am* statement.) What is the Lord speaking to you in your singleness right now?

Change:

Write some things you wish you could change in your life while dealing with being single.

Destroy any thought that does not line up to God's word, God's will or God's way.

Stop Signs Are Red for a Reason

"Ask for a sign from your God. Ask anything. Be extravagant. Ask for the moon!" Isaiah 7:11 (MSG). When we think of the color red, we think of a couple of things: danger, fire, and stop. Some of you are thinking about red nail polish, red lip stick, or for the guys, maybe a red pair of sneakers? Red is a very passionate color when it comes to the believer because it represents and signifies our sole existence— the blood of Jesus! In your singleness, I want you to know that the blood of Jesus sustains you while single! In your darkest moments of being single, never forget the blood of Jesus! For some of you, talking about the blood of Jesus means nothing to you anymore. It is the very essence of why you can wipe your tears at night, dust yourself off from listening to the lies of the enemy, and go about your day like you are not hurt or broken inside. The blood is our stop sign while being single! We are telling the enemy to:

> *Stop* messing with my mind.
> *Stop* feeding me lies.
> *Stop* telling me I'm not good enough.
> *Stop* saying that God doesn't have anyone for me.
> *Stop* saying I'll never find someone.
> *Stop* telling me that something is wrong with me.

The Word of God *cannot* work in your life if you are not in the Word of God. Don't you dare, in your Christian walk, forget that there is power in the color of red! Isaiah 7:11 (MSG) says to "ask the Lord your God for a sign, whether in the deepest depths or in the highest heights." Have you ever asked God to give you a sign?

We have all been in that place in life. You know that place of asking God questions like, "God, are they the one for me?" "What career path should I take?" "Am I going to the right church?" "God, are You even real?" "Does God really hear me?" You've been there, right? It's not just me, surely. The question I asked myself is do I really want to hear God's answers to all these questions? Many of us are frustrated in our faith because God usually doesn't answer in the way we want Him to. Think of it this way; you know how you ask for something on Christmas and then get the total opposite gift? We want God to answer our way. When He puts it in a package we don't like, we get disappointed.

Our unbelief places a distance between us and God. Psalms 10 says, "Why Lord, do you stand far off? Why do you hide yourself in times of trouble?" The enemy will continue to lie to you while single, and you will develop negative habits of talking down to yourself. You will begin to look in the mirror and believe the lies and all of the negative seeds that surround you! Don't forget who *loves* you! Don't forget who calls you beautiful one! Don't forget who gives you beauty for ashes!

Today, I want you to *start* affirming yourself with the Word of the Lord; *start* declaring that if it is God's desires for you to be in a relationship, He will make it happen; *start* praying that God will shut the mouth of the enemy; and *start* writing in your journal of what God says about you. I know this is familiar, but have you started to take matters into your own hands? Especially when it comes to your mentality? You've heard these things over and over again, so what are you going to do about it now? It's your time to *stop* listening to the lies and *start* speaking the truth. Stop signs are red for a reason! While in your singleness, what has the Lord said *no* to, and you've entertained them anyway? If the Lord says no, then don't do it! Doubt means don't, my friends! This week, I need you to do three things: Realize what's of God and what's not of God. Whatever is noble, right, pure, lovely, make a list of those things in your life. Then, reestablish your relationship with God.

Communication is key, right? Talking to God only when you need something or when you are in trouble will not cut it! Yes, He wants to hear from you in those times. He wants to hear from you daily. Just asking God for things like He is some genie in a bottle will not get His attention. Scripture says we must do three things—ask, seek, and knock. Last, we must remember the promises of God. We must wait for God's response, instead of jumping ahead with our own reaction. Relax, rest, and remember that God has your back!

Reflection Page

Single Until: Challenge/Confirmation/Change

My challenge:

Make a list of things that Challenge you in your singleness.

My confirmation for today:

(Start with an *I am* statement.) What is the Lord speaking to you in your singleness right now?

Change:

Write some things you wish you could change in your life while dealing with being single.

Look Both Ways

One of the very first lessons that you are taught in life is to look both ways when crossing the street. I was driving down the road, one day, and I heard the spirit of the Lord say, "Look both ways…" Holy Spirit then directed me to recall when I was younger when one of the first lessons I was taught before crossing the street was to look both ways.

Transitional seasons of your life are going to happen. Being promoted on your job, managing being a freshman to a senior, and from crawling to walking are all natural transitions that we embrace. I want to encourage you in this season of your singleness to look both ways! While you are dating, on your career path, or building friendships with your inner circle, I want you to look both ways. Why look both ways? Looking both ways ensures your safety.

During transition seasons, you are either going toward Christ, or you are going away from Christ. Every believer will have an Acts 9 "Damascus road" experience. While single, there will be many turning points that will force change. Turning points that will be so significant not only will change occur but choices will be made and your character will be defined. Which direction are you going right now in your life? Are you trying to cross the road of depression, defeat, or betrayal? Are you trying to cross the road to a new chapter in life? You must look both ways to make sure you don't stumble onto a path that was designed to hurt you. Be careful of distracted drivers! Or maybe you are the distracted driver. One of the leading causes of death on your Christian journey is a distracted driver. I want to encourage you in your singleness to not be a "distracted driver." I need you to focus in this season! Keep your eyes on your goals and your dreams! While you are on this road of being single, pay attention to the signs! I get so frustrated with so many of my friends when they ask me (the single one), "Well, how do you know if a person is the one?"

And my answer is always the same, "I have no idea..." But many people have said that when you know, you just know! I'll leave that right there. However, I definitely want to add on to how do you know if they are "the one:"

1. Are they leading you toward Jesus Christ or pulling you away from your relationship with Jesus?
2. Have you passed a sign called *peace*? Is there discord and dysfunction, and are you confused all the time with where you stand in the relationship? Christ and confusion do *not* coexist!
3. Are you ready to handle the heart that God has given to you?

Again, I am no expert! I am no counselor! Right now, I am literally in my prayer closet with some worship music playing and typing every single word that comes to mind. One thing I know about God is He is not a God that confuses us! As you try to cross this road to your purpose, just make sure that you look both ways! How do you make rational decisions? This simple concept—look both ways—will this take me in a direction toward Christ, or will this take me in a direction away from Christ? In your singleness, I just encourage you today to look both ways!

Reflection Page

Single Until: Challenge/Confirmation/Change

My challenge:

Make a list of things that Challenge you in your singleness.

My confirmation for today:

(Start with an *I am* statement.) What is the Lord speaking to you in your singleness right now?

Change:

Write some things you wish you could change in your life while dealing with being single.

Operation Destination

For I am confident of this very thing, that He who began a good work in you will perfect it until the day of Christ Jesus.
—Phillipians 1:6

Operation destination—the place to which one is going or directed. The ultimate pupose for which something is created or intended.

Who doesn't like going on vacations? Right now, you just pictured a beach or a rental cabin, didn't you? Maybe you can picture you and your friends on Jet Skis or singing around a campfire. Then, you will agree with me that vacations are carefully thought out way in advance. Gas prices, plane tickets, and the hassle of loading up your whole family or your friends for a couple of days sounds great in theory. But the planning of the trip is a whole different story. For some odd reason, the purpose of a vacation is to get away from the normal routine. We all want to leave and get away from the day-to-day stresses. The chaos of having to work, work, work. Regardless of the chaos of going on vacation. We desire to do something, plan something, vaction somewhere that will take our minds off of our curent situation.

I enjoy traveling. I will never forget this one trip I took to Texas. The flight was delayed due to mechanical issues. The flight was so full that, of course, *my* reschedule had to be the one not processed. I stayed in the Will Rodgers Airport all night. The next morning, it's time to load the plane. I was standing in line at the very end. Everyone from the night before had entered the plane, and I saw the cabin door shut. My heart dropped down in my stomach. I was tired from sleeping in the airport chairs; I was aggravated because they lost my reservation; on top of that, I lied to my parents that I was safe in Texas. I wasn't! I was stuck.

In your singleness, there are going to be moments when you are stuck. On your way to your destination, you may experience delays. Many of us on our spiritual journey have told God that we just want to get away from it all. We've packed our spiritual bags of guilt, shame, unforgiveness, lust, greed, and bitterness; and we want to get away. I want to ask you; what are you trying to get away from?

As we start off on Straight Street, something happnes between the start and finish of our singleness. We hit spiritual roadblocks of rejection, stumble across bumps of fear, hit potholes of lonliness, and get pulled over because we tried to speed past God with our own plans. Standing in line, waiting to get on the plane, and having the gate door shut on me was the best wake up call God could have given me. It wasn't my time to get on that plane, so I had to wait even longer. God was protecting me from something or someone that could have harmed me on the plane. Maybe God closed the gate door to see how I would react. Would I thank Him, or allow anger to win and yell at the gate attendants. Either way, I learned a lesson in my singleness. God is protecting me. God is saying it isn't my time to be in a relationship. God is checking my heart's posture and how I am reacting in this season. In our singleness, we don't always stay on Straight Street for long.

Our passion for Christ decreases, our zeal for Him is in lack, and if He doesn't answer our prayers on time, we start turning down a road called Back Street. You are not listening to the Back Street Boys on Back Street, I can tell you that! Back Street isn't just for the back slider! Back Street is a road traveled by many of us. If you are going through the motions of church, if you aren't really in your word or have an active prayer life, if you haven't grown closer to Christ in the last six months, you are definitely on Back Street. God is so gracious and soverign that He allows the flat tire not to harm us, not to stop us but to help us find the spare. You know, the spare tire that is hidden in various places in certain types of cars. The people that you cut off and dismissed were probably your "spare." The people that don't look like you, act like you, or worship like you, they were your "spare." You need to recognize the "spare tires" on your singleness joureny. Right now, I want you to picture yourself at a four-way stop. You have the road to the right of you. The road to the right of you will represent the right direction you need to go in to get closer with Christ.

The road to your left. That road will represent the direction the enemy wants you to go on. The road ahead of you is the direction God wants to encourage you to. The road behind you is the road that you leave your past behind, your guilt behind, and your shame behind. You are destined for greatness. Right now, in your singleness, you are destined for something big! Whatever road you may be traveling on in your singleness, please know that God needs to be your spiritual GPS. God wants to (G) guide you, He wants to (P) provide for you, and He wants you to (S) surrender to His will and His way.

Expectation. There needs to be a certain type of expectation for your singleness experience. You're not single and waiting just for nothing! No, ma'am! No, sir! If you have been single for a while, this is the perfect time to

1. invest in yourself financially and spiritually;
2. establish a foundation;
3. expect God to do whatever He wants to do in your life; and
4. figure out what you want out of life.

Place an *expectation* on your *faith* and expect God to bless your singleness experience in a mighty way!

Reflection Page

Single Until: Challenge/Confirmation/Change

My challenge:

Make a list of things that challenge you in your singleness.

My confirmation for today:

(Start with an *I am* statement.) What is the Lord speaking to you in your singleness right now?

Change:

Write some things you wish you could change in your life while dealing with being single.

For we walk by faith and not by sight! If you are feeling numb, dull, and unfulfilled because we are a generation that needs to "see it" before we "believe it." God is calling us to believe before we see! Walking by faith isn't easy, but it is necessary!

Over and Over Again

If you are feeling a little overwhelmed today, I want you to take a step back and just breathe! Take a time out of your busy day and just push pause on your life right now! I want you to turn to the book of Luke and read chapter 10:38–42.

> As Jesus and his disciples were on their way, he came to a village where a woman named Martha opened her home to him. She had a sister called Mary, who sat at the Lord's feet listening to what he said. But Martha was distracted by all the preparations that had to be made. She came to him and asked, "Lord, don't you care that my sister has left me to do the work by myself? Tell her to help me!"
>
> "Martha, Martha," the Lord answered, "you are worried and upset about many things, but few things are needed—or indeed only one. Mary has chosen what is better, and it will not be taken away from her." (Luke 10:38–42)

Some memories and some moments will forever be cherished in your mind. Maybe your favorite speaker said something a couple of years ago, and it just stuck to your bones! Today, one of my friends spoke life over me. They read this scripture and placed my name were Martha's name was. "You are worried and upset about many things, but few things are needed—or indeed only one."

Ask yourself these questions: Are you worried and upset about many things? Are you upset about not being in relationship? Are you worried that God doesn't have anyone out there for you? Are you upset that other people seem to be living their best lives on social media, and you are missing out? Are you worried people are looking at you in a different light because you haven't found anyone? This is the perfect time to be like Mary! *"Mary, who sat at the Lord's feet listening to what he said."*

This is what I want to forever remember for the rest of my days—*whatever I need is at the feet of Jesus!* When I am distressed and over life, everything I need is at the feet of Jesus! When people turn their backs on you, validation is at the feet of Jesus. Are you distracted by so much of this world that you are overwhelmed? Whatever you need today, it is at the feet of Jesus! I am sure that you have your quiet time, but has time become so routine that you are not hearing from God?

Mary was doing two things: sitting and listening. Sitting and listening is a posture that your heart must take on for the rest of your single life. It's one thing to sit at His feet, but are we listening to what God has to say? Rest is at the feet of Jesus. Restoration is at the feet of Jesus. The strategy to get you to the next season of your life is at the feet of Jesus.

One night, as I was teaching Bible study on this scripture, God downloaded this in my spirit. "Your personal distractions will delay your destiny, decrease your deliverance, and damper your dreams." Has school, your job, dating online, social media, and watching Netflix distracted you in this season? *"So then faith comes by hearing, and hearing by the word of God" (Romans 10:17).* Today, be reminded that whatever you need is at the feet of Jesus. Your posture for today is to *sit* at His feet. But not only sit but to listen. His promises are yes and amen! Today, find the promises that concerns your life and thank God in advance that He has not forgotten about you in your most distracted days!

Reflection Page

Single Until: Challenge/Confirmation/Change

My challenge:

Make a list of things that challenge you in your singleness.

My confirmation for today:

(Start with an *I am* statement.) What is the Lord speaking to you in your singleness right now?

Change:

Write some things you wish you could change in your life while dealing with being single.

The Season of Isolation

Isolation. The process or act of isolating or being isolate. *Separation.*

Key points to keep in mind. Isolation is (1) uncomfortable, (2) dysfunctional, and (3) tactic the enemy uses to separate.

Dear singles:

There will be some Friday nights and whole weekends that you are by yourself! *Accountability* is the only thing that's going to get you through some of those lonely nights! Please give yourself permission to be okay with going out with friends or in group settings. I believe the enemy uses isolation to tear us down, destroy our friendships, and disrupt our relationship with Jesus Christ. Be confident in going out with different groups of friends that will not make you feel like you are the fifth wheel. Do not allow the enemy to tell you that you are damaged! *You are God's* workmanship!

If you feel as though you are not as close to God as you once were, you are the one who has placed things before Him. God is the same today, yesterday, and forevermore! He doesn't love you any less. Change your priorities and stay focused on your purpose! In the season of loneliness and isolation, don't you dare get stuck there! There is going to be a period of time in your singleness that you are going to cry more than you pray. There will be days in which you are motivated because you are only responsible for yourself, and then, there will be days in which you are over being by yourself. The only way that you will get out of the season of *isolation* is through *accountability*! Be careful when choosing accountability partners. You can only help people that actually want to be helped.

In my life, I have experienced trying to be there for someone who was more hindering than helpful. Some people really are comfortable in their pits. Read Genesis 37:2–20 when you have a chance. I am not saying that we are exempt from pit experiences; I am saying that we do have a choice. You can't pull someone out of their pit if they won't grab hold to the rope of hope. Pit people are those comfortable in their depression. People in the pit enjoy pain because that's all they know. People in the pit wear a mask of positivity, when in reality, they are negative all the time. People in the pit enjoy their environment so much that they work up scenarios in their heads that make them physically sick. Pit people scream that they want to be helped, but honestly, they would rather sit in their misery. Don't forget, misery loves company. You need people around you in this particular season that will support you, motivate you, and comfort you.

James 5:16 encourages, "Therefore confess your sins to each other and pray for each other so that you may be healed. The prayer of a righteous person is powerful and effective." Here is how you know if you have chosen the right accountability partner; can you confess your sins to them? If you do not trust them, there is no way you are going to tell them what you are struggling with. You will struggle in your singleness; there is no doubt about it. Having accountability acts as a catalyst for strategic transformation and aids in your freedom in this season where you feel separated from Christ.

Be encouraged that nothing can separate you from the love of Christ. Confessing our sins one to another brings healing. Not just physical healing but emotional healing as well. God wants us to have life and have life more abundantly. Make sure you can confess to your accountability partner the good, the bad, and the ugly. Who keeps me *accountable*? List three people that will have hard conversations with you if necessary!

Reflection: Do I feel like I have separated myself from my friends? Am I by myself a lot lately? Have I separated myself from my relationship with Jesus? *Scripture that I can speak over my life to deal with my isolation* is Joshua 1:9, "Have I not commanded you? Be strong and courageous. Do not be afraid: do not be discouraged, for the Lord your God will be with you wherever you go."

Reflection Page

Single Until: Challenge/Confirmation/Change

My challenge:

Make a list of things that challenge you in your singleness.

My confirmation for today:

(Start with an *I am* statement.) What is the Lord speaking to you in your singleness right now?

Change:

Write some things you wish you could change in your life while dealing with being single.

Today, it is your choice of how this day will go! It is your choice to be happy! It is your choice to think positive! It is your choice if you want things to get better for your life! Choose today to dust yourself off, hold your head up, and move forward! Your attitude will determine this day! Happiness is a choice!

Earnestly

*Do not let your hearts be troubled. You believe
in God; believe in me as well.*

—John 14:1

Throughout the Word of God, we find words like *abide, dwell,* and
earnestly. Please do whatever you need to do to grasp the words in its
truest context. If you have ever been disappointed, discouraged, or
frustrated in your singleness, this may be the time to earnestly seek
and experience Jesus like never before.

I believe that many of us "*know of* Jesus," but barely *know* Him.
Knowing of Jesus in our minds and asking Jesus in hearts is the equiv-
alent to relationship and religion. What do I mean? Think about
people that we follow on social media. Think about the random fol-
lowers that are merely acquaintances. Half the people on our friend
list, we can barely call "friends." We *know of* them, but we don't *know*
them. We know that they have a puppy, a little sister, and they play a
sport because of what they post. So you know facts about some of the
people that you follow. That does not mean you know them personally. What I am saying is many people *know of* Jesus in the same sense
that He is just an acquaintance. We speak to Him when we are in
desperate need. We may like a few scriptures that make us feel good.
We only spend time with Him when we feel like it. Maybe you're like
me; you grew up in church, you can quote scriptures verbatim. You
even have a perception of what Jesus looks like. *You know of* Him.
But to truly understand the character of a person, you must spend
time with them. This is how we get to *know* Jesus. We know facts of
Jesus. We must spend time with Him and study the characteristics of

Christ. I believe when we find out *who He is*, we also begin to realize our true identity in Him.

"Continue earnestly in prayer, being vigilant in it with thanksgiving" (Colossians 4:2–6).

Earnestly in prayer means when you pray, you put your feelings aside for a moment. While spending time with God, you are determined not to move until God comes in your room, your office space, or your car while driving and speaks directly to you. Earnestly in prayer is seeking God *on* purpose for your purpose. Let me ask you this: when was the last time that you thanked God for being single? Be honest!

Here is what I want to challenge you with this week:

1. Thank God for this time of being single
2. Earnestly seek Him
3. Write down the characteristics of Christ as you spend time with Him

Your pursuit of Christ should be a top priority while you are single. Make a commitment this week that you will spend time with Jesus at least thirty to forty minutes a day. I don't want you to place this on your "to-do" list. I want you to be intentional about earnestly seeking the face of God. As always, we make time for the people that are important to us. How important is it for you to get to know your Creator?

Reflection Page

Single Until: Challenge/Confirmation/Change

My challenge:

Make a list of things that challenge you in your singleness.

My confirmation for today:

(Start with an *I am* statement.) What is the Lord speaking to you in your singleness right now?

Change:

Write some things you wish you could change in your life while dealing with being single.

Maximizing Your Time with Jesus

Teach us to number our days that we may
gain a heart of wisdom.

—Psalm 90:12

I want you to start with a declaration today. Say this out loud: "I will start making time for Jesus! Today, I will pray for wisdom and gain the knowledge I need for not only my future relationship but with my relationship with Christ!" Maximizing your time with Jesus requires a little more effort than what you are doing right now! I'm not saying that reading your daily devotional is not enough. I want to encourage you to change up your routine so that it doesn't become just a check mark. Challenge yourself for the next twenty-one days to make your quiet time more intentional, intimate and more special.

You will never know God as your healer if you have never experienced healing for yourself. You will never know God as your provider if you have never had to struggle. The same God that commanded *peace* over the storm is the same God that can calm any high waves that are raging in your life right now. What I have learned in my singleness is that God is my comfort and my peace! When I want to give up on dating, God reminds me of His commitment and His constant pursuit of me.

While you are single, this is the perfect time to maximize your time with Jesus! Are you praying for the companion that God wants to release to you? By now, while in your singleness, you have probably heard people say, *"Maybe you haven't met them yet because they aren't ready."* Sweetie, maybe you aren't ready. Maybe your relationship with Christ has been inconsistent. Your devotion to God's word and God's will has been frustrating because God is not a top priority. God wants all of your attention. I am not saying that God is holding your future spouse hostage or anything of the sorts. We serve a jealous God. We need to ask God for wisdom right now in our singleness.

Lastly, are you asking God to *prepare* you in this time for your future spouse? Please understand this; God is a keeper! What does that mean? God will not give up on you. Regardless of what you have done! "The Lord is your keeper; the Lord is your shade on your right hand" (Psalm 121:5). God watches over us! Think about it. When no one else was there to hold you at night, God was there! When no one else wanted to listen to you, God did. Although you may be frustrated that it is taking forever for your person to come, God is still right beside you! Time is precious. We can't lack the understanding or wisdom that God wants to give to us in this season! We also can't lack knowledge considering the characteristics of Christ. Once we figure out who *He* is to us, He will begin to transform us into the very person that someone else needs us to be to glorify God and to advance the kingdom. Today, we are praying that we may gain a heart of wisdom in this season of singleness.

Reflection Page

Single Until: Challenge/Confirmation/Change

My challenge:

Make a list of things that challenge you in your singleness.

My confirmation for today:

(Start with an *I am* statement.) What is the Lord speaking to you in your singleness right now?

Change:

Write some things you wish you could change in your life while dealing with being single.

No one deserves their heart to be played with! If someone is interested in you, they will definitely pursue you. Keep this in mind: the enemy doesn't attack, but he definitely distracts! There shouldn't be any confusion when it comes to someone pursuing you; especially if they have Jesus living inside of them. They will love what God loves! They will honor God by guarding your heart!

Conversations with the Right Connections

Iron sharpen iron, and one man sharpens the face of his neighbor.
—Proverbs 27:17

Have you ever met a person in your life, and something just automatically clicked? Think about your relationships at your job or at school. You cannot tell me that you talk to everyone about everything! If you do, please let me know the secret. I do not let everyone have access to my personal life. But you know, your circle, your people, your squad—the ones that have your back? A couple of people just popped in your mind, right? I believe that God uses right connections to impact our life in such a way that leaves us better, stronger, and wiser to chase after our destiny. Right connections are also called divine connections. This type of relationship changes your life and makes such an impact on your heart that should ultimately strengthen your pursuit of Jesus Christ. I can't tell you enough that God does not want us to *do* life alone. Divine connections are so powerful that if you didn't have that person in your life, doors wouldn't have opened, strategies would have not been discussed, and you would have been going through the same cycle if they didn't pray you through your most mundane times of life.

I am sure, by now, you have some people in mind. If not, think about the people that challenge you to chase after your dreams and not to quit on the vision that God has given you. Think about the person that encourages your potential and not your past. Think about the person that has been in your life for a while. The one that knows your very being. They are connected to your life for the calling that is on your life. Conversations with the right connections are so important in this time of your singleness because you are going to need them on your very high highs and your very low lows.

You know those "high highs" of singleness; you just met a great guy or girl, made a real connection with him/her, and of course, you want to share it with someone! And *your* person just gets you. You don't have to explain anything to them. Then you have your very "low lows" of singleness. The nights you might cry yourself to sleep. The person you go to when you hit rock bottom because your heart just feels like it has been ripped out of your chest. The Bible says, "Be completely humble and gentle; be patient, bearing with one another in love." I believe that I said this before, but I will say it again; people are in your life for seasons, reasons, and lessons. The people that you are divinely connected to understand your moral compass. They understand your purpose in life. Divine connections catapult you into kingdom thinking.

One of my favorite Bible verses explains divine connections this way: "Two are better than one, because they have a good return for their labor: if either of them falls down, one can help the other up" (Ephesians 4:9–10). You need people in your corner that want to see you succeed. You need people on your team that will pick you up when you fall down. To put it simply, the music artist, Ciara, came out with a song entitled "Level Up." The chorus of the song says the same thing over and over again, "Level up, level up, level up, level up…" Right connections are going to help you "level up" in your personal and professional life. One thing I know for certain, God provides you with key people that makes life worth living.

Your challenge for this week is to recognize your divine connections that God has sent. Remember that divine connections do not manipulate. They support the vision God has given you, they will not allow you to quit, and they promote great growth in your personal and professional life. Tonight, in your prayer time, thank God for your divine connections. Pray that God will send you people that will connect you to the kingdom of God.

Reflection Page

Single Until: Challenge/Confirmation/Change

My challenge:

Make a list of things that challenge you in your singleness.

My confirmation for today:

(Start with an *I am* statement.) What is the Lord speaking to you in your singleness right now?

Change:

Write some things you wish you could change in your life while dealing with being single.

Toxic cycles stop when you are connected to divine connections.

Access Denied

If you remember, throughout the Bible, there are many instances that the Lord gave access to certain types of people to get them from one point to the other. You remember Moses parted the Red sea; God gave him access to the resources and the boldness that he would need. He gave Joshua access and specific instructions to march around the wall of Jericho, and by obeying those instructions, the walls came down. You remember David? David was given access to kill a giant and, later on, become a king! God granted him access. Ruth was a widower placed in her future husband, Boaz's, field, and guess what? You're getting it! God gave her the green light, if you will! She had access.

Access is defined as a means of approaching or entering a place. I want to encourage you today that in your life right now, you have access to power. His name is Jesus. *"Therefore being justified by faith, we have peace with God through our Lord Jesus Christ: by whom also we have access by faith into this grace wherein we stand, and rejoice in hope of the glory of God" (Romans 5:1–10).* Please read other translations of this verse. I just wanted to get this word, *access*, into your spirit today. I want you to understand that God wants to open doors for you in this season of your life. God wants you to experience His love, favor, and overflow in this season of your singleness.

Reading the rest of this scripture, it lets me know that we will go through stages in our singleness. Not only our singleness but our lives. Romans 5:1–10 says that there is going to be a suffering stage of our singleness. But our suffering now is going to help us endure. When we endure, it is going to help us build character, which gives us hope. When we endure those lonely nights, when we push through being alienated, we are going to receive hope. Once you get through this season of your singleness, it is your time to help someone and give hope to someone else. You can't throw in the towel right now; don't you dare give up on dating, especially if it is a desire of your heart. I want you to ask yourself why are you struggling in your singleness right now? Is it because you have the wrong people around you? Are you sliding into DMs, trying to get someone's attention?

Please understand that *everyone* and every thought should not have access to your life. *Repeat after me*: "Everyone and every thought should not have access to my life." When you allow negativity, pessimism, and dormant thoughts to enter and corrupt your mind, you are giving access in becoming stagnant in your singleness. The Word of God says that "life and death are in the power of your tongue." Think of it this way; whenever you log into a computer and forget a password. You only have about three tries before it says, "Access Denied." We must be very careful of what we allow to enter and exit into our life. Everyone and everything should not have a password to your mind and your heart. I want to encourage you to evaluate what is entering into your mental, spiritual, and physical space. Who are you getting advice from when it comes to addressing your singleness? Is the advice that is given to you godly counsel, or is someone giving you advice from a worldly perspective?

Kingdom singleness can only be cultivated by kingdom mindsets. When you are discouraged in your singleness, who is speaking life over you instead of death? What I want to encourage you with today is that you have access to the presence of God. I was so discouraged one season that I just knew that God was either mad at me or disappointed in me. Everyone around me was posting engagement pictures, baby announcements, and even one of my best friends stopped talking to me due to an engagement. I was very careful who I let know how discouraged I was. Some people like to kick you while you're down. And if you are discouraged in this season of singleness, look around you. Who has access to your heart right now? Some of you are dating the wrong person right now! That's a pretty bold statement, right? If there is any confusion in your current relationship/ friendships at this very moment, stop allowing confusion to have access in your life. If it is a toxic relationship in which one minute, they like you, and the next minute, they are ghosting you, this is the time to have hard conversations with yourself and with others.

Remember that by faith, we have been made acceptable to God. It is also by faith that we have access to Jesus Christ.

On the reflection page read Romans 5:1–10, and write down keywords that stand out to you. Make a list of people that have entered into your life.

Reflection Page

Single Until: Challenge/Confirmation/Change

My challenge:

Make a list of things that challenge you in your singleness.

My confirmation for today:

(Start with an *I am* statement.) What is the Lord speaking to you in your singleness right now?

Change:

Write some things you wish you could change in your life while dealing with being single.

The X Marks the Spot

For where your treasure is, there your heart will be also.
—Matthew 6:21

Can we go back to a time of when playgrounds and juice boxes were our favorite things to do? The opposite sex either had cooties, or they were our best friends. Think back when you were young; you had your best friends, which was pretty much your whole kindergarten class! Use your vivid imagination right here. Girls, take yourself back to a place of being the princess of your castle. Your bedroom floor instantly turned into fire or water. Your pillows became swords and shields. Guys, you know that we are waiting for our knight in shining armor, right? Let's remember your backyard and finding a piece of paper covered in chocolate pudding, some crayon lines, and a large, red X marking the treasure's location.

The *X* marked a spot where someone had buried something of value! This will hopefully encourage you today that you—yes, you—have been marked by the hand of God! There are no physical marks on your body. However, the Word of God says He knows every strand of hair on your head. He knows every detail of your life. He knows every thought that has been said. He knows our entire being. We are His, and He is ours, and we have much value in the eyes of God.

Now, it is God in us who makes us stand firm in Christ (2 Corinthians 1:21–22). He anointed us, set His seal of ownership on us, and put His Spirit in our hearts as a deposit, guaranteeing what is to come. Today, let us thank God for His deposit! Thank You, God, for depositing peace into my spirit. Thank You, God, for giving me joy in this time of being single. Thank You, Lord, for making a deposit of Your Spirit into my heart. Thank You, God, for giving me hope in my singleness.

Think of it this way; the more deposits you make at your bank or the more change you place in your piggy bank, at the end, it is going to continue to add up. Second Corinthians encourages us that God has set His seal of ownership on us. Daily, in our singleness, God makes valuable deposits in our spirits that encourage us to continue to keep going when we want to give up! When you invest in a person that you have interest in, you are making a deposit of your time, your mental wellness, and your heart. Your treasure is connected to your heart. We are God's treasure, and we are connected to the heartstring of God. This should place a little hope back into your heart. This should encourage you that you matter to God. Not only do you matter to God, but you have been marked by God and have great value. Maybe, right now, your treasure is clothes, career, or looking for your significant other. Someone once told me that if you really want to see where someone's heart was, look into where they spend the most money. Ouch!

We are all on a journey right now! We want to find the right career, the right partner, the right friends, the right church, etc., and if we are not careful, we will find ourselves off course! We are treasures in God's eyes! Although the person God has for you hasn't found you, it just means you are marked! And the right person will find you at the right time! Today, where is your treasure? I encourage you to draw a treasure map of your heart on the reflection page. Today, figure out the requirements of your hand and burry them deep in God's heart.

Reflection Page

Single Until: Challenge/Confirmation/Change

My challenge:

Make a list of things that challenge you in your singleness.

My confirmation for today:

(Start with an *I am* statement.) What is the Lord speaking to you in your singleness right now?

Change:

Write some things you wish you could change in your life while dealing with being single.

Trusting God in Transition

I wrote this blogpost back in 2015. Now, in my thirty-two years of singleness, this is what I have learned so far on my journey of being single. I'm going to try to keep this as simple as I possibly can. But what I need is for you all to focus on these words: *transition*, *process*, and *change*.

Transition. The process or a period of changing from one state or condition to another. What I have found is that we are in a constant state of *transition* in life and especially in our singleness. "God is striding ahead of you. He's right there with you. He won't leave you. Don't be intimidated. Don't worry" (Deuteronomy 31:8, MSG). We transition from crawling to walking. We transition from middle school to high school. We transition from a bottle to a whole steak. Depending on our age, some of us change careers like we change our clothes. Some of us transition from college right into the married and adult life.

There is a constant choice that we must continue to make throughout life. And as a believer, you will find yourself in a *constant process of change*. (Many people would call this the "season" of *transition*.) The season of transition can be difficult if you do not have someone or something developing and pushing you into what God has called you to be. I wanted to write down some of the things that I was going through in my singleness to help someone else. If this devotional helps one person, it will be worth it. What I know for certain is *all transition* processes are different. Some seasons of transitions are harder than others. I found myself in the hardest season of transition this year. You know that place between a rock and a hard place? Yes, I was there. Am I still there? I still may be. However,

I have found that some seasons of life we place ourselves in and the *transition* process might just be one of those constant states.

Transition equals process equals change. What I have found out, however, is that *in* the process of transition, you will begin asking, "So what's the plan, God? What is it that You want me to learn while I am single?" Some of us can't hear from God because we don't like what He is saying (S. Ditto).

God told me that one night, He said, *"You probably can't hear from Me because you don't want to listen to what I have to say."* This slapped me in my face. He punched me in my gut. Some of us have what I like to call *"spiritual selective hearing."* That is when you hear what you want to hear. We want to hear that we are blessed. We want to hear that Jesus loves us. But we have a problem when God says, "Die to yourself." That's just the *real* and intense conversations that we need to remember; God's sheep know His voice. Listen, you know your parent's voice, right? If you were in a grocery store, in a crowd of people, and if your mother called your name, you would recognize her voice. It is the same way with Jesus. The more you spend time with Jesus, the more you recognize His voice. Over and over again, we are reminded to renew our minds; put on a new self; think of things ahead; ask, seek, and knock; pick up your cross daily; die to self; love thy neighbor as yourself; trust in the Lord with our whole heart; guard your heart; seek first the kingdom of God; etc. (You get it!) All those things I just mentioned require you to *focus* on the *process.*

The *process* requires *change* and *development.* For some, *change* requires you to be uncomfortable. When we are uncomfortable, we don't step out, and we do the total opposite of what God has called us to do. Instead of going, we *stop.* Instead of growing, we stay stagnant. Instead of believing—well, it's not that we don't "believe," but we throw up our hands, and we tell God that we give up! I do not want you to give up on your journey of being in a relationship.

1. The process of transition strips you of your identity. If you don't know *who* you are, *whose* you are, *where* you are going, *what* you are supposed to be doing in life, the sea-

son of transition will come and rob you of your joy and fulfillment.

2.   Transition will make you think twice about moving ahead. Now, you know what God has promised you. You know you serve a *big* God! You know for a fact God has a plan for your life. But because of the season of transition, you either get stuck in the season, or you take two steps back into settling. Failure knocks at your door, depression creeps through your window, and isolation seems to be sleeping in your bed. Transition will do that to you!

3.   Transition will stretch you to *greater*. One thing I do know about transition is that transition will cause you to grow. You will figure out who you really are in Christ. Transition will cause your *faith* to be stretched. It will open your eyes to things you would have never seen because of your flesh.

Singleness does not define who you are. God is not holding back any blessing concerning your life. In this time of singleness, He is preparing us to trust Him while we transition. It's a process of change. Kingdom singleness requires constant change. Are you preparing for what you have been praying for? Begin to pray for a strategy while single and in transition.

The question of the day: are you trusting God in your transition?

Reflection Page

Single Until: Challenge/Confirmation/Change

My challenge:

Make a list of things that challenge you in your singleness.

My confirmation for today:

(Start with an *I am* statement.) What is the Lord speaking to you in your singleness right now?

Change:

Write some things you wish you could change in your life while dealing with being single.

You can either quit or keep going, continue to worry or begin to worship, push panic or pray about it, give (it) to God or handle (it) by yourself.

Prepare for what you are praying for.

About the Author

Shajuana R. Ditto's debut devotional, *Single Until*, comes from personal experience. She has coached volleyball for the past ten years at three different high schools. She is a pastor, youth and young adult minister, and motivational speaker. For thirty-two years, she has never gone on one single date. Through *Single Until*, her hopes are to encourage and to empower her audience through her personal experiences of being single. She is passionate about reaching this next generation one page at a time through *Single Until*. Relationships are important to us which makes relationships important to God. What happens when you find yourself stuck in the middle? The middle is a place of compromise and questioning God. The place where your value is dependent upon validation from others. This singleness journey is about taking a moment to reflect and realize that God has more for your life. It is a process you can grow through to get to the very people, place and things that God desires for your life. Ditto believes that God is going to restore the relationships in your life. She wants to give you a strategy of hope that through *Single Until* individuals will find themselves more confident, bold and encouraged while being single. It's time to resurrect godly relationships and restore hope back into what is important to God. What is important to God is the capacity to become who God has called you to be and to love who God has called you to love.

At the age of seventeen, she was called into the ministry and hasn't looked back. She has preached across the state of Kentucky, encouraging the next generation to pursue their relationship(s) with Jesus Christ and that there can be hope while living single.